T0381940

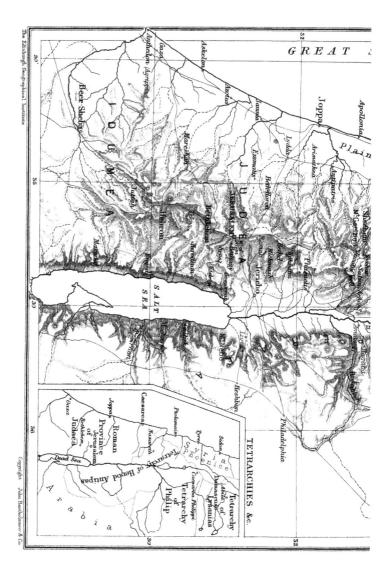

GREAT

Gaza

Anthedon (Agrippias)

Ascalon

Azotus

Beer Sheba

I D U M E A

Joppa

Apollonia

Plain

Jamnia

Arimathea

Lydda

Emmaus

Bethletepha

Thamna

Gophna

J U D E A

Maresha

Bethsura

Adora

Beth-zur

JERUSALEM (Aelia Capitolina)

Bethlehem

Herodium

Engedi

Tekoah

Hyrcania

Betharamphtha

Medeba

Juta

Hebron

Maon

Carmel

SALT SEA

Masada

Zoar

Callirhoe

Machaerus

Heshbon

Philadelphia

TETRARCHES &c.

Gaza

Joppa

Caesarea

Roman
Province
of
Jerusalem
Bethlehem
Judaea

Dead Sea

Nazareth

Ptolemais

Tyre

Sidon

S y r i a
P H O E N I C E

Caesarea Philippi

Libia of
Abilene
Tetrarchy of
Lysanias

Tetrarchy
of
Philip

Tetrarchy of Herod Antipas

A r a b i a

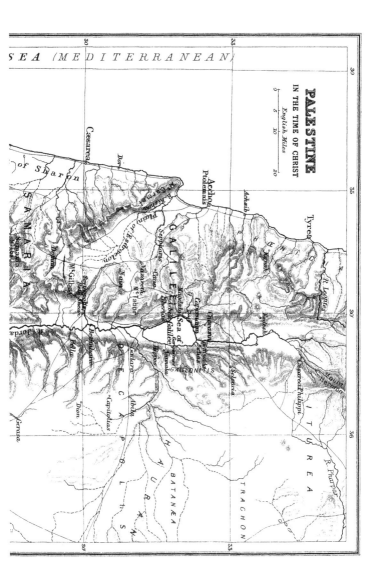

SEA (MEDITERRANEAN)

PALESTINE
IN THE TIME OF CHRIST

English Miles
5   0   5   10   20

THE GOSPEL ACCORDING TO

ST MARK

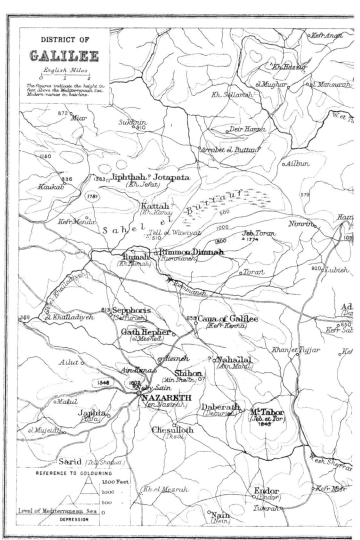

DISTRICT OF

GALILEE

English Miles
0   1   2

The figures indicate the height in
feet above the Mediterranean Sea.
Modern names in hairline.

Kefr Anan

Kh. Hazur

el Mughar · el Mansurah

Kh. Sellameh

W. el Hamam

872 · Miar

Sukarin ·510

Deir Hanna

1150

Arrabet el Buttauf

Ailbun

336 · 1363 · Jiphthah? Jotapata
(Kh. Jefat)

Kaukab

1781

Kattah?
(Kh. Kana)

B u t t a u f

500

379

Kefr Menda

S a h e l   e l

Tell el Wawiyat
510

1000

Jeb Toran
▲ 1774

1500

Nimrin

108

Rumah
(Kh. Rumah)

Rimmon Dimnah
(Rummaneh)

Toran

820 · Lubieh

Canal Khallatiyeh

el Khalladiyeh

Errumaneh

389

513 · Sepphoris
(Seffurieh)

Gath Hepher
(el Meshed)

858 · Cana of Galilee
(Kefr Kenna)

Khan et Tujjar

Ad
(Da
650
Kefr Sab

Ket

Ailut

er Reineh

? Nahallal
(Ain Mahil)

Ain Mana ·

Shihon
(Ain Sha'in) ?

1548   1602 · Neby Sain

NAZARETH
(en Nasirah)

Daberath
(Deburieh)

Mt Tabor
(Jeb. et Tor)
1843

Japhia
(Yafa)

Matul

Chesulloth
(Iksal)

el Mujeidil

Sarid (Tell Shadud)

REFERENCE TO COLOURING

1500 Feet
1000
500

Level of Mediterranean Sea   0

DEPRESSION

Kh. el Mezrah

W. esh Sharrar

Endor
(Endor)

Kefr Misr

Tumrah

Nain
(Nein)

The Edinburgh Geographical Institute

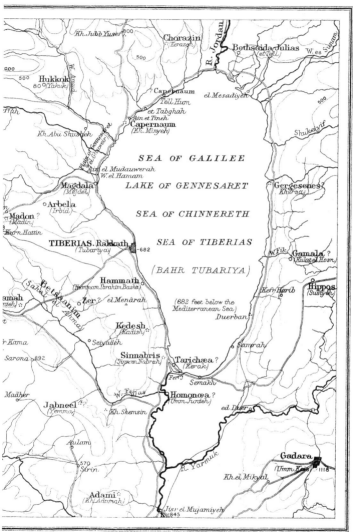

SEA OF GALILEE

LAKE OF GENNESARET

SEA OF CHINNERETH

SEA OF TIBERIAS

(BAHR TUBARIYA)

(682 feet below the
Mediterranean Sea)
Duerban

Chorazin
(Kerazeh)

Bethsaida Julias
(et Tell)

W. es Semak

Kh. Jubb Yusef

500

500

Capernaum
Tell Hum
et Tabghah
Ain et Tineh
CAPERNAUM
(Kh. Minyeh)

el Mesadiyeh

Shukeiyif

500

Hukkok
80°/Yakuk

600

500

Kh. Abu Shusheh

Tilah

Tell el Oreymeh
Flood of Gennesaret

Ain el Mudauwerah
W. el Hamam

Gergesenes?
(Khersa)

Magdala
(Mejdel)

Arbela
(Irbid)

Madon?
(Madin)
Kŭrn Hattin

TIBERIAS. Rakkath
(Tubariya)

682

Gamala?
(Kulat el Hosn)

W. Fik

Hammath
(Hammam Ibrahim Basha)

Kefr Harib

Hippos
(Susiyeh)

Zer?

el Menârah

Betsd. Janim

Sahel el Ahma

amah
ideh

Kama

Kedesh
(Kadish)

Samrah

Seiyadeh

Sarona

892

Sinnabris
(Sinn en Nabrah)

Tarichæa?
(Kerak)

Madher

Jabneel
(Yemma)

W. Fejjas

Kh. Shemsin

Ferd

Semakh

Homonœa?
(Umm Juneieh)

ed Duer

R. Jordan

R. Jordan

Gadara
(Umm Keis)

1118

Aulam

Sirin

570

R. Yarmuk

Kh. el Mikyal

Adami
(Kh. Admah)

Jisr el Mujamiyeh
845

St MARK

THE REVISED VERSION

EDITED WITH INTRODUCTION AND NOTES
FOR THE USE OF SCHOOLS

BY

Sir A. F. HORT, Bart., M.A.,

ASSISTANT MASTER AT HARROW SCHOOL,
FORMERLY FELLOW OF TRINITY COLLEGE, CAMBRIDGE,

AND

MARY DYSON HORT

(Mrs GEORGE CHITTY)

CAMBRIDGE
AT THE UNIVERSITY PRESS

1903

CAMBRIDGE
UNIVERSITY PRESS

University Printing House, Cambridge CB2 8BS, United Kingdom

Published in the United States of America by Cambridge University Press, New York

Cambridge University Press is part of the University of Cambridge.

It furthers the University's mission by disseminating knowledge in the pursuit of education, learning and research at the highest international levels of excellence.

www.cambridge.org
Information on this title: www.cambridge.org/9781107680067

© Cambridge University Press 1903

First published 1903
First paperback edition 2014

A catalogue record for this publication is available from the British Library

ISBN 978-1-107-68006-7 Paperback

PREFACE BY THE GENERAL EDITOR
FOR THE GOSPELS AND ACTS.

THE Revised Version has to some extent super-seded the need of annotation on the Gospels and Acts, so far as the meaning of words and phrases is concerned. But the present Edition will, it is hoped, serve a good purpose in drawing the attention of young scholars to the importance of some of the changes made in that Version.

Another aim is to present in a clear and intelligible form the best and most approved results of recent theological work on these books.

The General Editor takes this opportunity of noting that, as in *The Cambridge Bible for Schools*, each writer is responsible for the interpretation of particular pas-sages, or for the opinion expressed on any point of doctrine. His own part is that of careful supervision and occasional suggestion.

ARTHUR CARR.

October, 1903.

CONTENTS.

	PAGE
INTRODUCTION	vii–xxvii
A. Origin of the Gospels . . .	vii
B. The Writer and his Book . .	xi
C. The Historical Setting of the Gospel History	xvii
ANALYSIS OF GOSPEL	xxviii
TEXT AND NOTES	1–117
INDEX TO NOTES	118–120

MAPS.

| Palestine . . . . | *Frontispiece* |
| District of Galilee . . . . . | *after* p. xxviii |

Available for download in colour from www.cambridge.org/9781107680067

INTRODUCTION.

A. ORIGIN OF THE GOSPELS: RELATION OF ST MARK'S GOSPEL TO THE OTHERS[1].

Features distinctive of each of the four Gospels.

THE Gospel is contained in four books, two called after apostles, St Matthew and St John, two after companions of the apostles, St Mark, the companion of St Paul and of St Peter, and St Luke, the companion of St Paul. The same Person is brought before us, in the main the same story is told four times over. But there is no mere repetition, for each writer sees the life which he is describing from his own point of view, and no two of them were writing for the same class of readers. Thus St Matthew's interest lay in the past; he wrote to shew his own countrymen, the Jews, how the life of Jesus had fulfilled all that was written in the Law and the Prophets concerning the Messiah. St Mark lives in the present: he writes for Romans (see below, p. xiv), and gives them a living portrait of a living man. St Luke, influenced by the far-reaching aspirations of his master, St Paul, looks forward to the day when all flesh shall see the salvation of God, and, writing in the first instance for his own countrymen, the Greeks, brings before them One who was fitted to be the Saviour of all nations in every age. St John, writing

[1] Adapted from the *Cambridge Companion to the Bible.*

long after the other three for the instruction of the Christian Church, gazes on the eternal mysteries which had been brought to light by the revelation of the Word made flesh.

Corresponding to these differences between the writers of the Gospels, and between the classes of readers to which they were originally addressed, there is a difference between the features in the character of the Lord which stand out most prominently in each. Thus the first three help us to see in Jesus the perfect Son of man, St John shews us the same Jesus as the perfect Son of God.

St Mark's Gospel follows the outline of the public preaching of the apostles.

It is important to remember that, although the Gospels stand first in our New Testament, this order does not represent the order in which the books were written. In the earliest age of Christianity there were no written Gospels, because the need for them had not arisen. The facts on which the apostles laid most stress in the earliest public teaching were the Death and Resurrection of the Lord, those facts which were of the first importance in the message which they had to deliver. While the memory of His words and works was still fresh, there was no need of a written record. But we learn from Acts i. 22 that it was regarded as essential that an 'apostle' should have personal knowledge of the life and teaching of Jesus during the whole period between the Baptism of John and the Ascension: and it is this period which was embraced in the earliest form of the written Gospel. St Mark traces 'the beginning of the gospel of Jesus Christ' (i. 1) from the advent of the Baptist: his book as we have it is incomplete (see n. on xvi. 8), but we may well believe that, had the conclusion of it been preserved, it would have carried on the narrative up to the Ascension.

The other Gospels in various ways supplementary.

St Mark's Gospel then represents the Gospel story in its earliest and most elementary form, and gives such facts about the life of Jesus as Gentile Christians would wish to know. But it soon became necessary to prefix to this story of the Ministry of Jesus some account of His birth, and other events connected with it: and such accounts we have in the Gospels of St Matthew and St Luke. The outline of the Gospel story was now complete. It remained for St John to supply important details which were omitted by the first three evangelists, to throw new light on the gradual revelation of Christ's Person in His human life, and generally to present His life and teaching in a 'theological' aspect to meet the growing needs of the Church: it was becoming necessary by that time not merely to accept the record of His life as historical fact, but to think more deeply about its meaning as revealing the eternal purposes of God.

The Synoptic Problem.

The record given in the first three Gospels is called the 'Synoptic' narrative, and the three writers are called the 'Synoptists,' because (as distinguished from St John) they give the same 'synopsis' or general view of the life of Christ. It is obvious that the three narratives have much in common, that they not merely tell the story of the same events, but to some extent tell it in the same way, or even in the same words; so that the writers cannot be thought to have written in entire independence of one another. On the other hand it is equally clear that each of the three books contains things which are not found in the others: indeed they do not always agree in the details, when they are telling the same story. In fact their independence of one another is quite as striking as the strong similarities between them. Our difficulty then is to account for these two opposed facts, to frame a theory as to how these books came to be written, which will account at the same time for the dependence and for the independence of the three narratives: and we have practically no means of information except the books themselves. This difficulty is called the 'synoptic problem.' An examination of passages found in St Mark in common with St Matthew, and in some cases with St Luke, gives the impression that in very many instances the words which St Mark gives us lay before the other synoptists, each of whom has modified them from his own standpoint, sometimes by compressing the story and sometimes by adding further details from sources of his own. Similarly, when certain passages common to St Matthew and St Luke are compared, it appears that there was another common source of information which both of these evangelists used, but not St Mark.

The further question arises whether, if these inferences are correct, the 'common sources' which were drawn upon by the evangelists existed in the form of *written* documents, or whether they consisted of an '*oral*' tradition as to the words and works of Jesus. In the latter case the histories, from being constantly repeated (before they were written down) in the instruction of Christian converts, may well have become, as it were, fixed in a certain form, so that even the same words, to a great extent, were used whenever the story was told, and were consequently preserved when it came to be written down. At present however most scholars incline to the first theory, that of primitive *written* records: the terseness of the narratives and the general absence of comments, such as would naturally fall from a teacher's lips, point rather in this direction.

In any case our Gospel of St Mark probably closely represents (if it is not identical with) the earliest form in which the apostolic tradition of our Lord's life was committed to writing: and it is not unlikely that this document was actually seen and used by St Matthew and St Luke.

Accordingly, it is of first-rate importance that we should get as clear an understanding as possible of the meaning of St Mark. It is, however, important to remember that St Matthew and St Luke must have had access to other sources of information, which may well be equally early and authentic.

B. THE WRITER AND HIS BOOK.

The life of St Mark.

If it be assumed[1], as it may be with tolerable certainty, that the John Mark mentioned in the Acts is the same person as the Mark of St Paul's epistles and as the author of the Gospel, we may put together the following fragmentary biography of the evangelist. His Hebrew (Aramaic) name was John, and he adopted the Roman *praenomen* Marcus as a second name. His mother's name was Mary; she was a Christian and a person of some position in the Church at Jerusalem, as we see from what is said of her household in the account of Peter's escape from prison (Acts xii. 12—17). We there see that John Mark was probably already intimate with Peter. This is the earliest certain mention of him; he is not mentioned in the Gospels, though it has been conjectured that he was one of the Seventy, and with more likelihood that he was the 'man' of Mark xiv. 13, who guided the two disciples to the house where they were to prepare the Passover, and the 'young man' of Mark xiv. 51, 52 (see notes), who was present at the arrest in the garden of Gethsemane: if these conjectures could be accepted, it

---

[1] See Col. iv. 10 and cf. Swete's commentary, chapter on 'The personal history of St Mark.' Hastings, *D.B.*, John Mark.

would seem that the Last Supper was taken at his mother's house, the same house to which Peter turned on his escape from prison.

We next hear of him in Acts xii. 25, where it is said that Barnabas and Saul took him with them from Jerusalem to Antioch, on their return thither after administering the relief fund sent from Antioch for the Christian poor at Jerusalem: this was in 45 or 46 A.D. At this time Saul was rather second in command to Barnabas than leader of their missionary enterprises, and we learn from Col. iv. 10 that Mark was a relation of Barnabas: this was doubtless one reason for his selection, and he may have already proved useful to the apostles at Jerusalem. He accompanied Barnabas and Saul on the first missionary journey, and after being with them in Cyprus, sailed with them to Pamphylia. On this expedition it is said (Acts xiii. 5) that he acted as their 'attendant,' i.e. apparently as a sort of courier. At Perga in Pamphylia he left the apostles and returned to Jerusalem, his home[1] (xiii. 13). This 'desertion,' as St Paul regarded it, led subsequently to a breach between that apostle and Barnabas, since, when they were starting on the second missionary journey (Acts xv. 36), Barnabas wished again to take Mark with them, but Paul refused, and the two apostles travelled separately, Mark accompanying Barnabas to Cyprus, which was the latter's own country. It is clear however that Mark had been allowed to rejoin the apostles at Antioch during their stay there previous to the second missionary journey, and it would seem that it was only as a companion in missionary travels that St Paul objected to him. From this point we hear no more of him in Acts. There is nothing improbable in the tradition that he proceeded from Cyprus to Egypt: there he is said to have founded the Church at Alexandria ; legend goes on to

[1] For a suggestion as to the reason of his conduct see Ramsay, *St Paul the Traveller*, &c., Chap. v.

say that he there suffered martyrdom, and that his remains were eventually taken to Venice, of which he became the patron saint. For this story, interesting as it is, especially in connexion with the romantic history of Venice, there is no authority.

Our only authentic information as to his later life is gathered from the epistles of St Paul and St Peter, and we know nothing certain about his death. From Col. iv. 10, 11, and Philem. 24 (written at the same time as Col.), we find that he was at Rome during St Paul's first imprisonment there, and it is evident that there was now complete harmony between them: he is called in Col. iv. 11 one of St Paul's 'only fellow-workers...of the circumcision.' After this he seems to have gone to Asia, as in 2 Tim. (iv. 11), the latest of St Paul's epistles, addressed to Timothy at Ephesus during Paul's second imprisonment at Rome, just before his death, Timothy is told to 'pick up' Mark and bring him to Rome, and it is added that he is 'serviceable for ministry.' We thus gather that his place in the early Church was that of a practical industrious subordinate, a character which is borne out by the early traditions presently to be mentioned, and by the simple unpretending tone of his Gospel.

Again, in St Peter's first epistle, written also probably from Rome (1 Pet. v. 13), Mark is spoken of as 'his son,' and it is implied that he too was then at Rome. We have seen that the intimacy began in early times at Jerusalem; and the phrase 'my son' apparently indicates that he was a favourite 'pupil.' It is considered likely that St Paul's death occurred earlier than St Peter's, and that this epistle was written in the interval: in that case it would seem that Mark (with perhaps others of St Paul's circle) transferred his services to St Peter. It is with St Peter that tradition especially connects his name: he is called Peter's 'interpreter,' and this he may well have been in a literal sense, if Peter was not familiar with Greek. It is asserted that he wrote a record of Peter's preaching, consisting of the doings and sayings of Christ: the description given of this work applies closely to our 'Gospel of St Mark' (see below, p. xvi). The traditions which give us these facts vary in some particulars, but the earliest of them go back a long way and may be accepted as trustworthy. The later traditions appear to go too far in asserting that Mark wrote in any sense at the *dictation* of Peter. It was this connexion with Peter's name that probably gave to St Mark's Gospel its authority in the early Church.

Mention may be added of the curious epithet 'stump-fingered' which is applied to St Mark by some fairly early authorities. The meaning may be either that he had a natural defect in the hand or hands, or that he had suffered some kind of 'mutilation' from an accident or otherwise.

The contents and style of the Gospel.

All that we are able to gather about his later life goes to support the view that his Gospel was written in the first instance for *Roman* Christians, and it contains just those things which such converts would wish to know, a vivid sketch of the personality of Jesus as He 'went about doing good' in Galilee, and instructing His disciples for their future work, and of the attitude of rulers and people towards Him; and a full description of the circumstances of the crowning scenes of His earthly life (see below, p. xvi). St Peter's speech to Cornelius (Acts x. 36—40) supplies just such a 'table of contents' for our Gospel.

The main characteristic of St Mark's style is extreme simplicity of language. 'Simple' sentences predominate, strung together with such connexions as 'and straightway.' There is little of elaborate syntax, and, if the construction of a sentence is difficult, it is generally not because of complexity, but because it is broken in a free, almost

conversational way: hence 'sense-constructions' and
parentheses are not infrequent. There is no 'word-paint-
ing' or rhetoric, the facts are left to tell their own story.
Very few words are used, yet the story is not bald, because
brief as is the account, no picturesque feature is omitted:
hence we often find in St Mark an added detail which
brings the picture more vividly before our eyes than the
accounts of the same event by St Matthew or St Luke.
He shares with the other synoptic writers a strange power
of suppressing his own personality and feelings, and an
extraordinary reserve in refraining from comment on the
momentous events which he describes.

Its first readers.

It is evident that the book was written in Greek, and is
not a translation. It contains a good many Latin words,
but they are mostly such as must have become current
among Greek-speaking subjects of the Roman Empire,
being for the most part words for Roman coins or military
terms. The readers whom St Mark had in view would
be Greek-speaking converts, especially Christians of the
Church at Rome; those to whom St Paul and St Peter
in succession had preached. Such readers would desire
just such a plain statement of the main outward facts
of our Lord's life as St Mark gives: they would not be
specially interested in Him as a Jew, and they would
not be fully acquainted with Jewish customs or ways of
thought. Hence he explains for their benefit the Aramaic
words which he occasionally introduces, and the allusions
to Jewish customs or beliefs, while he does not, like St
Matthew, appeal to a knowledge of Jewish literature and
prophecy.

The plan of the Gospel.

The Gospel falls into well-defined sections: the two
principal ones are (1) a selection of typical incidents of

Jesus' ministry in Galilee, derived doubtless from St Peter's
'reminiscences,' and (2) a full account of the last days at
Jerusalem, for which the writer evidently also drew on
other sources of information: it must be remembered that
Jerusalem was his own home. Between these two main
sections comes a very brief sketch of Jesus' ministry in
Peraea (which is fully treated by St Luke): the work
opens with an introduction on John the Baptist's preaching—leading up to Jesus' baptism and the opening of
His ministry in Galilee—and ends with an (incomplete)
account of the events of the morning after the Resurrection.

Within each section the events appear to be arranged
in what the writer considered to be their chronological
order, so far as his information went. Thus in the section
on the Galilean Ministry what is said of our Lord's methods
of preaching clearly shews a natural sequence. We learn
that *first* He preached in the synagogues of Galilee, *then*
to a larger audience by the lake-sides or among the hills,
then that He began to address the people at large in
'parables,' and *finally* that He devoted Himself more and
more to the special training of the Twelve. But, though
a certain order is thus discernible, it would be a mistake
to consider either this Gospel or any of the others as by
itself constituting a 'Life of Christ.'

Traces of St Peter's influence.

The influence of St Peter may be detected not only in
those details about him which St Mark alone gives, but in
significant omissions. Thus e.g. the stories of the rebuke
to Peter and of his fall are told circumstantially, the account
of the Transfiguration, as describing St Peter's confusion,
could hardly have come from anyone else, and on several
occasions he is named by Mark and not by the other
evangelists who record the same incidents: while on the

other hand things which might seem to exalt his dignity
are omitted, such as the great promise made to him as
the representative of the apostles (Matt. xvi. 17—19), and
the account of his walking on the sea (Matt. xiv. 28—32).

C. The Historical Setting of the Gospel History[1].

The interval between the Testaments.

It is impossible to understand the conditions under
which our Lord's life was passed without knowing something of the history, religious and political, of the Jews in
the period between the end of the Old Testament history
and the beginning of the Gospel history. In our Bibles
St Matthew immediately follows Malachi, and we are apt
to forget how wide is the gap. The latest event recorded
in the last historical book of the Old Testament took place
more than four centuries before the coming of John the
Baptist, a period as long as that which divides our own
time from that of the Wars of the Roses. In that period
great changes took place, so that the Jews of the New
Testament must be regarded as very widely different from
the Jews of the Old. Indeed the history of the Jewish
people during that time covers what is in many ways the
greatest period of their national life, and includes some
of the most characteristic exhibitions of Jewish character
and Jewish ideas: it is a period conspicuous for striking
events, for new developments of religious thought, and for
elaborate organization of internal government. It is to
that epoch that we must look for explanation of the
political and religious ideas of our Lord's contemporaries,
as we find them depicted in the Gospels. Thus there is
little in the Old Testament itself to account for the intense

[1] Adapted mainly from the *Cambridge Companion to the
Bible*.

feeling of the nation's right to independence, the developed hopes of a future life, and of the coming of the great Deliverer, the Messiah, the punctilious reverence for the letter of the Law shewn by Scribes and Pharisees, or the peculiar views of the Sadducees. In fact the religion of the Jews in the time of Christ (and religion with this nation was always closely bound up with politics) was not either in its higher or its more popular form the religion of the Israel of the books of Kings: it was that religion as modified, chastened and enriched by the experience of the Captivity at Babylon, the stern discipline of the Return, and the manifold changes and chances of 400 years of struggle for national existence. The thoughts and hopes which filled the minds and stirred the imaginations of the contemporaries of Christ were more directly moulded and inspired by the reforms of Ezra and the exploits of the Maccabees than by the heroes and prophets of an earlier generation. Without some knowledge then of this period we cannot properly enter into our Lord's attitude or that of His apostles to the Law of Moses, or the Jewish sects of His time, or the Roman government: nor again can we understand the attitude of His contemporaries towards Him, and the popular hopes which His career excited or disappointed.

The beginnings of important changes are seen in the books of Ezra and Nehemiah. We there see how widely the Jews who returned differed from their fathers of 50 years before. Then they were under kings, but now they were to be ruled by priests. Again, whereas before the Captivity they had been constantly torn by divisions, given to idolatry, careless of the Law, freely mixing with other nations, now on the other hand they were united as a nation, they were zealous in the worship of the one God, and almost servile in their devotion to the Law, and their revived patriotism took the form of a narrow and rigid exclusiveness with regard to all foreigners. National pride was fostered by the institution of a new Feast, Purim, which commemorated a great national deliverance. This new Israel was largely the work of Ezra, the first 'scribe,' and Nehemiah, the zealous if narrow-minded reformer. A brief sketch is subjoined of the period thus inaugurated: it is clear that new forces were at work, which could not but produce important developments. But a period so rich in incident necessarily loses in interest when it is compressed into a few paragraphs.

For convenience the whole period between the Testaments may be divided into three sections.

1. *The period of subjection and silent growth.*

[From the death of Nehemiah (B.C. 415) to the accession of Antiochus Epiphanes (B.C. 175).]

Throughout this period Israel played no independent part in history. At first the Jews were under governors appointed by the kings of Persia, under whose rule they had passed when Cyrus conquered the Babylonian Empire during their captivity at Babylon. The Persian Empire, which he founded, was subdued after about 170 years by Alexander of Macedon, and Palestine therefore became part of his vast dominions. Those dominions were divided at his death in B.C. 323, and the Jews became by turns subject to Egypt and Syria : their country lay between these two powers and was often the battlefield of their wars.

But, though thus dependent first on one power, then on another, the Jews did not lose their consciousness of being a nation, and in many ways 'silent growth' was going on.

It was then that arose the institutions, the sects and the forms of religious thought which we meet with in the New Testament. In religion the idea of the Unity of God gathered strength, while the hope of the Messiah took more definite shape; the expectation of a future life became clearer, and a doctrine of angels was developed. And closely combined with their religious hopes was the fervid spirit of patriotism which has made the Jews the most distinct among the nations of the earth.

Meanwhile it is likely that they were left by their successive masters tolerably free to govern themselves: the high-priesthood passed from father to son, and the high priest was practically a petty king. Few of these rulers were distinguished: one of them, Jaddua, is said to have had a remarkable interview with Alexander the Great, who received him well and granted favours to the Jews in different parts of his dominions: the greatest of them in the eyes of the later Jews was Simon the Just, of whose dignity and splendour an ideal portrait is given in the 50th chapter of Ecclesiasticus, written long afterwards. This picture shews at least the importance of the Temple in the life of the nation, and the impressiveness of this almost unique form of government.

(*The Jews outside Palestine and the origin of the Septuagint.*)

Connexion with Egypt produced important consequences. In B.C. 320 one of the Ptolemies (Greek kings of Egypt) took Jerusalem, the refusal of the inhabitants to fight on the Sabbath making the capture easier. Thousands of Jewish captives were taken to Alexandria. There the Septuagint (LXX), the first written translation of the Old Testament books, presently appeared, being made for the benefit of Jews to whom Hebrew was now a dead language (the Jews of Palestine now spoke, not Hebrew, but a Syrian dialect called Aramaic). The Version gets its name from a tradition which relates that Ptolemy Philadelphus (285—247 B.C.), being anxious to secure a translation of the Jewish laws for his famous library at Alexandria, applied to the high priest Eleazar of Jerusalem, who sent six elders from each of the tribes of Israel to Egypt: these 72 translators were royally entertained, and produced their work in 72 days. In this story the kernel of historical fact seems to be that the Pentateuch was translated in Alexandria in the reign of Ptolemy Philadelphus, probably in the first instance to meet the needs of the synagogues of Greek-speaking Jews. Most of the rest of the books of the Hebrew Canon were added before 132 B.C. The whole was probably complete and in general circulation before the time of the apostles. This Greek Bible became the Bible of a vast number of Jews: the benefit to them may be compared to the benefit which our forefathers received when the Bible was first translated into English and so became the property of all who could read, and not merely of the learned few: the later Jews did not necessarily know the original Hebrew any more than a modern Englishman necessarily knows Anglo-Saxon or a modern Greek the language of Homer. It is from this translation that the Old Testament quotations in the New Testament are mainly taken: hence it cannot be neglected in our study of the New Testament. Moreover, since Greek was the language of a large part of the Eastern world, this translation did more than anything else to break down the barrier between Jew and Gentile: Jewish and Greek ideas now met and began to react on one another. This intermixture of Jew and Greek was further promoted by the establishment in Palestine of Greek settlements. Without realizing these things, we could not understand how a Gospel written by a Jew came to be written in Greek, and why it is that in the Gospel story Greek influence meets us constantly. (See n. on Galilee, pp. 59, 60.)

The Syrian kings of this period (see above) also shewed consideration to the Jews, to many of whom they granted the privileges of citizenship. This explains how in the

Christian Era so many Jews were Roman citizens, since the wise Romans after their conquest of Syria continued the Syrian policy of indulgence to their subjects. The ultimate result of the wars between Egypt and Syria (see above) was the victory of Syria under Antiochus the Great: in his reign Palestine, as part of the defeated Egyptian empire, became a province of Syria (B.C. 203). In the reign of his successor internal factions at Jerusalem caused the intervention of the Syrians; the king's envoy attempted to plunder the Temple, and, according to the story, was miraculously repelled. This crisis was the beginning of a new state of things.

2. *The Maccabean rule.*

Now began a period of fierce struggle, in striking contrast to the previous period of (on the whole) quiet subjection to indulgent masters. An attempt was made by a party of the Jews themselves to introduce Greek customs at Jerusalem, and this attempt was stoutly resisted by the 'exclusive' party. The result was that Antiochus Epiphanes invaded the country in 169 B.C., pillaged and profaned the Temple, slew or took captive thousands of Jews, and posted a Syrian garrison on the Temple hill. He then proceeded to a violent persecution of the religion of Jehovah, the object of which was to force the Jews to adopt the paganism of the rest of his vast empire. The first step was to be the erection of altars to Zeus throughout Palestine. Then came the resistance. The first active protest was made by an aged priest called Mattathias, who slew both the sacrificers and the royal officer who had been sent to establish the heathen worship. Further persecution followed, but for a considerable time heroic resistance was led by members of the family of Mattathias, generally called the Maccabees.

The first and greatest of these was Judas Maccabaeus,

who won many victories over the Syrians, restored the desecrated Temple, conquered also jealous neighbours, such as the Edomites and Ammonites, and even made a treaty with Rome. The struggle was carried on by Judas' brothers, one of whom, Jonathan, for his services to one of the Syrian kings against a rival, was made by him high priest. This was an important step in two ways: it set the precedent, afterwards followed by the Romans, for the *appointment* of the high priest by the power that ruled Palestine (instead of the office being, as formerly, hereditary); and it gave to the family of the Maccabees (also called from an ancestor the Asmonean house), the nominal, as well as the actual authority over their countrymen. Israel had never since the time of Solomon taken so high a place among the nations as during the rule of Jonathan. With the next reign, that of Simon, the nation became practically independent, for the first time since the Captivity.

In B.C. 135 John Hyrcanus became high priest and chieftain: he conquered the Samaritans, the formidable neighbours of the Jews, and destroyed their rival temple on Mount Gerizim. His eldest son, Aristobulus, was the first to take the title 'king of the Jews.' Another of his sons, however, Alexander Jannaeus, incurred the hatred of his subjects, and his death was followed by a time of confusion, in which the power of the Asmonean house came to an end, and another great family, that of the Herods, came to the fore.

3. *The Herodian dynasty.*

There was now a quarrel for the high-priesthood between Hyrcanus and a second Aristobulus. The former was supported by Antipater, father of Herod the Great, an Idumean, i.e. of the Edomite race which had from olden times been bitterly hostile to Israel. At Antipater's instigation, Hyrcanus, after once resigning his claims, revived them, and pleaded his cause before Pompey, who was then (B.C. 63) in the East, having recently conquered Syria and made it a Roman province. Pompey restored Hyrcanus, but he became henceforth little more than a puppet in the hands, first of Antipater, and afterwards of his son Herod. Aristobulus had attempted some resistance, whereupon Pompey besieged Jerusalem. Once again the scrupulous observance of the Sabbath gave an advantage to the enemy. A terrible massacre followed the capture of the city, and the Jews were scandalized by an act of sacrilege: Pompey entered the Holy of Holies, expecting to find some visible sign of the mysterious Eastern worship; in the words of the Roman historian he found nothing (*vacuam sedem et inania arcana.* Tac. *Hist.* v. 9).

Then the Romans settled the country: it was divided into five separate governments. At the same time a number of Jewish captives were carried to Rome and there formed a colony which was afterwards to have important consequences in the history of the Jews and of the Christian Church. Antipater was made a Roman citizen and *procurator* of Judaea, and was succeeded in that position by his son Herod, while the feeble Hyrcanus sank into insignificance. One more desperate effort to recover the lost position of the Asmonean family was made by Antigonus, the son of Aristobulus. The immediate result was that Herod fled to Rome: but there he ingratiated himself with Antony and Octavian, and was recognized by them as 'king of the Jews' in B.C. 40. Jerusalem was once more captured by Roman armies. Herod ruthlessly massacred the party opposed to him; Antigonus was scourged and crucified. Herod then further strengthened his position by marrying Mariamne, a daughter of the old Asmonean house. Her brother, Aristobulus, was made high priest by Herod and then murdered by his orders. He also compassed the death of the aged Hyrcanus, then of his wife Mariamne, and lastly of her two sons. The story of his passionate remorse is well known[1]. By such atrocities the house of Herod was secured against the Asmonean family.

One of his latest crimes, the massacre of the infants at Bethlehem, is known to us only from St Matthew. The Gospel history only touches the closing years of his reign, and we gather thence little about him except the terror of his name. But he was remarkable for other things besides his hideous crimes. To the Greek and Roman he was perhaps the most striking figure in the Eastern world. He was the friend and ally of Augustus, from whom he had received a kingdom, and towards whom he displayed a profuse and noble gratitude. His rule was inspired by the example of Rome, and it was to Rome that he sent his sons to be educated under the roof of a distinguished noble, Pollio, the friend of Vergil and of Augustus (see Verg. *Ecl.* iv). To the Greek he appeared as the lover and patron of Greek authors and philosophers. He was appointed perpetual president of the great Olympic festival, which he had re-endowed and restored to its former splendour. He introduced the games of Greece and the shows of the Roman amphitheatre into the cities of Palestine, and adorned those cities with buildings in the style of Greek architecture. By the Jew he must have been regarded in various aspects. Fierce hatred must for the most part have pursued the Idumean upstart, who ruled by the overthrow and slaughter of the beloved family of the Maccabees; who had massacred the Sanhedrin and the learned men of Israel; who in his youthful campaigns had slain by the sword thousands of Galilean patriots; who did violence to the ancient spirit of Jewish exclusiveness by foreign innovation; and whose cruel and capricious despotism, supported by a barbarian soldiery, brought fear and insecurity upon Israel.

[1] See S. Phillips, *Herod, a tragedy*, for a powerful modern presentation of the story.

On the other hand there were some who, in the powerful prince who had conciliated the favour of the successive rulers of the world, and who by the steady support of Rome had placed the Jewish race high among the nations of the earth, thought they saw the promised Deliverer of Israel. Hence the formation of a 'Herodian' party which meets us in the Gospels.

But by far the greatest work of Herod as king of the Jews, and one which with some went far to atone for his crimes and cruelty, was the rebuilding of the Temple at Jerusalem. This magnificent structure, its courts, and its stately colonnades, created genuine admiration and enthusiasm, and did much to give prestige to the Herodian dynasty.

Subjection to Rome.

From this sketch it is clear that by the time of our Lord's appearance the influence of Rome in Palestine had become dominant. Much as the Jews, or many of them, resented this domination, it must be remembered that the Roman form of government was the wisest and best known to the ancient world. It secured good order, it was in the main just, and it left the subject nation in many respects free to govern and develop itself. What the Jews most resented was the system of taxation: see n. on ii. 14.

It remains to note what changes of rulers took place during the period covered by the Gospel history. Herod the Great died very shortly after our Lord's birth, and his 'kingdom,' by permission of the Emperor, was divided into three parts, ruled by his sons with the title of 'tetrarch.' Philip became tetrarch of Batanaea, a district N.-E. of the Lake of Galilee: this region was visited by our Lord late in His Galilean ministry, when we find Him in the neighbourhood of Caesarea Philippi, the city which Philip had rebuilt and called by his own name: see n. on viii. 27.

Herod Antipas ruled Galilee and Peraea (see Map of Palestine): he is the Herod of whom we hear most in the Gospels: he beheaded John the Baptist, and our Lord was sent before him by Pilate (Luke xxiii). Archelaus was tetrarch of Judaea, but he governed so cruelly that the Emperor Augustus shortly deposed him, and made Judaea a Roman 'province': i.e. it was henceforth governed by a *procurator* (more important provinces were governed by *legati*): this meant that the Jews were brought directly under Roman rule and had to submit to the presence of a Roman garrison. The political capital of Judaea was Caesarea Stratonis on the coast, and troops were also posted at Jerusalem in the tower Antonia close to the Temple. This change took place in A.D. 6: hence Judaea had been a Roman province for several years when our Lord's ministry began: Pontius Pilate, by whom He was tried, was the fifth who had held the office of *procurator*. He gave great offence to the Jews by his contempt for their religious feelings, which partly explains his anxiety to conciliate the people at the time of the Trial: see n. on xv. 1.

Thus in attempting to realize the conditions under which our Lord's human life was passed we must take into account (1) the influence of the Roman government, which had existed in various forms for nearly a century at the time when His ministry began: and (2) the character and feelings of the Jews, as moulded by the varied history of their nation in the four centuries since the Captivity. In the above sketch of that history something has been said to explain the origin of the beliefs and prejudices which we meet with in the Gospels. For further explanation see the notes on the Pharisees (ii. 16), the Sadducees (xii. 18), the Zealots (iii. 18), the Scribes (i. 22), the 'kingdom of God' (i. 15), the synagogue (i. 21): the limited jurisdiction of the Sanhedrin is illustrated by the account of the Trial of Jesus.

ANALYSIS OF ST MARK'S GOSPEL[1].

INTRODUCTION.

I. 1—13.

(*a*) Title. (*b*) Preparatory Mission of John.

(*c*) Preparation of Jesus for the Ministry.

PART I.

INCIDENTS OF THE GALILEAN MINISTRY.

I. 14—IX. 50.

a. In Eastern Galilee. [I. 14—VII. 23.]
Three sections.

β. In Northern Galilee. [VII. 24—IX. 50.]
Two sections.

PART II.

SKETCH OF JOURNEYS IN PERAEA AND GALILEE.
X. 1—53.

PART III.

THE LAST WEEK.
XI. 1—XV. 47.

CONCLUSION.

THE RESURRECTION.
XVI 1—8.

[APPENDED SUMMARY ON THE RESURRECTION.
XVI. 9—20.]

[1] See headings in Notes for detailed Analysis.

THE GOSPEL ACCORDING TO

ST MARK.

I. 1–13.

INTRODUCTION, including (*a*) Title, 1. (*b*) Preparatory Mission of John, 2–8. (*c*) Preparation of Jesus for the Ministry, 9–13.

(*a*). 1. *Title.*

THE beginning of the gospel of Jesus Christ, the Son 1 of God.

(*b*). 2–8. *Preparatory Mission of John.*

Even as it is written in Isaiah the prophet,   2
  Behold, I send my messenger before thy face,
  Who shall prepare thy way ;

(*a*). 1. *Title.*

[*Matt. iii.* 1–12. *Luke iii.* 1–18. *John i.* 15–34.]

I. 1. This *v.* is either a general title to the book or indicates John's ministry as 'the beginning of the good news.' Cf. Acts i. 1. **the gospel.** In the N.T. the word = 'good news.' Later, the meaning was 'a book recording the good news.' **Jesus.** A common Jewish name, given to our Lord at His birth (Matt. i. 21, 25) with special significance, as it means ' Lord,' ' Saviour.' **Christ**. A title, meaning 'the Anointed,' and representing the Heb. 'Messiah.' The two names are not used together in the *narrative* of the gospels.

(*b*). 2–8. *Preparatory Mission of John.*

2. foll. To grasp the meaning of the passage read first 4, 'John came......,' then 'Even as it is written.' **Isaiah** (xl. 3). The only O.T. passage quoted by St Mark himself. See Introd. p. xv. Cf. Matt. iii. 3 ; Luke iii. 4 ; John i. 23. The passage is from the great prophecy Is. xl.–lxvi., now generally attributed to a 'second Isaiah,' who wrote during the Captivity. It was taken by the Jews as referring to the Messiah, though its first reference was to the Return from Babylon. The words 'Behold, ...thy way' are not however from Isaiah, but from Mal. iii. 1. Possibly Mark quotes from a collection of Messianic prophecies.

3   The voice of one crying in the wilderness,
     Make ye ready the way of the Lord,
     Make his paths straight ;

4 John came, who baptized in the wilderness and preached
5 the baptism of repentance unto remission of sins. And
  there went out unto him all the country of Judæa,
  and all they of Jerusalem ; and they were baptized
6 of him in the river Jordan, confessing their sins. And
  John was clothed with camel's hair, and *had* a leathern
  girdle about his loins, and did eat locusts and wild
7 honey. And he preached, saying, There cometh after me
  he that is mightier than I, the latchet of whose shoes
8 I am not worthy to stoop down and unloose. I baptized

---

3. Make straight. As the road was cleared and levelled
before a conqueror's advance.

4. the wilderness. The W. of Judaea, near the Baptist's
early home (Luke i. 39). The actual site was probably the
southern ford of the Jordan, 5 m. above its mouth, on the high-
road to Jerusalem from the East[1]. See also John i. 28, iii. 23.
preached. See Luke iii. 2–14 for the character of his preaching.
baptism of repentance. The washing was the outward *sign* of
repentance.   **unto remission,** i.e. repentance, 'change of
heart,' *led to* forgiveness. John, like the earlier prophets, insisted on *moral* reform, not on religious observances.

5. Note the general interest in this revival of prophecy.
were baptized. The Jews already admitted proselytes by baptism. They would understand therefore that John's rite admitted
them to some new life which needed fresh initiation[2].

6. The traditional prophet's dress, see Zech. xiii. 4. Also
cf. Luke i. 15, the Nazirite vows. The Jews expected Elijah to
reappear as the Messiah's forerunner (see Mal. iv. 5 ; Matt. xi.
14).   **camel's hair.** A rough cloth woven from the hair.
locusts. Still eaten in the desert, and said to taste like shrimps.
wild honey. See 1 Sam. xiv. 25–27.

7. John preached first repentance, and then the coming of
Christ. See also Luke iii. 15. John declared himself unworthy
to act even as His bath-slave, i.e. to perform the service of the
lowest menial in a household. Cf. Christ's own action John xiii.
4.   **the latchet,** i.e. 'the thong' of the sandals ; 'latchet' is
the old English word for 'lace.'

[1] Hastings' *Dictionary of the Bible*, 'John the Baptist.'
[2] Cf. Edersheim, *Life*, i. 273, 274, Appendix xii, (vol. ii.).

you with water; but he shall baptize you with the Holy Ghost.

(*c*). 9–13. *Preparation of Jesus for the Ministry.*

And it came to pass in those days, that Jesus came 9 from Nazareth of Galilee, and was baptized of John in the Jordan. And straightway coming up out of the water, he 10 saw the heavens rent asunder, and the Spirit as a dove descending upon him : and a voice came out of the heavens, 11 Thou art my beloved Son, in thee I am well pleased.

---

8. baptize you with the Holy Ghost. A startling metaphor, but intelligible to those familiar with such passages as Joel ii. 28, "I will pour out my spirit upon all flesh," part of a Messianic prophecy.

(*c*). 9–13. *Preparation of Jesus for the Ministry.*
[*Matt. iii.* 13–17. *Luke iii.* 21, 22. *John i.* 32–34.]

9. in those days. Probably at the end of the year 26 A.D. The following was a sabbatical year, when the people, freed from agricultural duties, would be able to follow a new teacher[1]. **Nazareth.** The village stood on the hills of S. Galilee, not far from the Plain of Esdraelon, the battlefield of O.T. history, crossed by the chief high-roads to Egypt, Jerusalem, and the East. Thus our Lord's boyhood was not passed in entire seclusion from the busy world[2]. The natural route for Jesus would have been across this plain to Beth-shean, and thence down the Jordan Valley. See Map.

10. And straightway. Mark's usual phrase to introduce a new incident. **as a dove.** Perhaps a symbol of God's mercy towards mankind, as at the Flood, Gen. viii. 10, 11. The dove appears nowhere in the O.T. as an emblem of the Holy Spirit. See Luke iii. 21 for further detail.

11. a voice. Such a voice was heard again at the Transfiguration (Matt. xvii. 5) and in the Temple Courts in the Last Week (John xii. 28). **beloved.** The adjective is used in the Septuagint for the Heb. word translated 'only-begotten.' It was also a recognized title of the Messiah. Cf. also Gen. xxii. 2. **I am well pleased.** Possibly an echo of Is. xlii. 1, lxii. 4, both recognized as Messianic prophecies. Jesus recognized John as a true prophet, and submitted to be baptized by him (1) as a devout Israelite, who must 'fulfil all righteousness' (Matt. iii. 15)

---

[1] This edition follows the chronology adopted by Dr Sanday in Hastings' *Dict. of the Bible*, 'Jesus Christ.'
[2] G. A. Smith, *Hist. Geog. of the Holy Land*, 432–435.

12 And straightway the Spirit driveth him forth into the
13 wilderness. And he was in the wilderness forty days
tempted of Satan ; and he was with the wild beasts ; and
the angels ministered unto him.

I. 14—IX. 50.

PART I. INCIDENTS OF THE GALILEAN MINISTRY, arranged
    in two groups. *a*. In Eastern Galilee. *β*. In Northern
    Galilee. Each of these may be subdivided, *a* into three
    sections, *β* into two.

FIRST SECTION. [i. 14–iii. 12.]

A. (*a*). 14–38. *First preaching in Galilee. Group of miracles.*

14 Now after that John was delivered up, Jesus came
15 into Galilee, preaching the gospel of God, and saying,

---

and submit therefore to whatever the prophet might decree as
essential : (2) in order to declare the continuity of His own work
with that of the Baptist : (3) to share Himself in an ordinance
which He intended His followers to maintain (Matt. xxviii. 19) :
(4) that thus He might be consecrated in a special way for the
great work of His ministry. 'In Him was no sin,' so that in His
case there needed no 'washing away' of sinfulness. From this
time forward His 'call' is manifest to the nation, to whom John
points Him out as the true 'Lamb of God,' John i. 29–34.

12. the wilderness. We are not told where this was. The
Jews believed that evil spirits specially haunted the deserts.

13. forty days. Cf. the account of Elijah's retirement,
1 Kings xix. 8. **the wild beasts.** The hyenas and jackals
of the desert. This picturesque detail is characteristic of Mark's
style. Details of the Temptation are given Matt. iv. 1–11 ;
Luke iv. 1–12. Attempts to produce failure in faith and misuse
of powers entrusted to Him were the weapons tried vainly
against Jesus by the 'Adversary' (the lit. meaning of the word
'Satan'). See refs. to later temptations, Mark xiv. 35, 36 ;
Luke xxii. 28. **angels ministered.** Cf. Elijah's experience,
1 Kings xix. 5. See also Heb. i. 14, and 1 Tim. iii. 16.

A. (*a*). 14–38. *First preaching in Galilee. Group of miracles.*

[*Matt. iv.* 12–22, *viii.* 14–17. *Luke iv.* 14–41, *v.* 1–11.

John iv. 43–54.]

14. There is a gap in time between the events of *vv.* 13 and
14, corresponding to the Ministry in Judaea and the incidents
immediately following, recorded by John (ii. 13–v.). The period

The time is fulfilled, and the kingdom of God is at hand :
repent ye, and believe in the gospel.

And passing along by the sea of Galilee, he saw 16
Simon and Andrew the brother of Simon casting a net

---

omitted by Mark probably covered rather more than a year.
John was delivered up. A reference to his imprisonment by
Herod Antipas, see vi. 17–29. That whole passage belongs *in
time* to this place, for John was imprisoned after the Ministry in
Judaea, and before this first tour in Galilee.   **into Galilee.** On
His way Jesus passed through Samaria. See John iv. 1–42 for
a full account. 'Galilee'='circle,' i.e. 'district.' Its area was
about that of Oxfordshire and it comprised the lower hills of the
Lebanon range and the Plain of Esdraelon. It was thickly
populated and fairly fertile, and was crossed by the great high-
roads from Damascus and the East to Phoenicia and Egypt.
Many Gentiles (Greek-speaking Syrians in our Lord's time) were
settled in the district, whence its original name 'Galilee of the
Gentiles.'

15. Cf. our Lord's message with the Baptist's (i. 4). The
new proclamation completed the first, and added the message of
'good tidings' to that of 'repentance.'   **the kingdom of God.**
Probably the phrase was familiar, though the Jews' conception
of its meaning was very different from our Lord's, which He
gradually unfolded to His hearers in discourse, exhortation, and
parable. Material riches, power, and glory, were expected by
the Jews as the signs of Messiah's kingdom. Jesus showed them
its spiritual character, and the error of these expectations. See
iv. 11–32 (parables of the Kingdom), x. 24, 37 (misconceptions of
it). Also Matt. v. 1–20, the Laws of the Kingdom.   **believe
in the gospel.** Belief *in* the 'good tidings' leads to belief *on*
Christ.

16. Here Luke (iv. 16–30) places the preaching and rejection
at Nazareth. Mark inserts it later (vi. 1–6).   **sea of Galilee.**
Called also Chinnereth, Gennesaret, and Tiberias. It is a lake
13 miles long by 8 broad, and is nearly 700 ft. below the level
of the sea. Its shores were then the busiest part of Palestine,
being the centre of a great fishing industry, supplying fish to all
parts of the Roman Empire, and bringing hundreds of traders to
the district. Our Lord therefore chose for the beginning of His
Ministry the most crowded centres of population[1].   **Simon and
Andrew.** They had been already 'called' (John i. 35–37, 40)
and had been on a short tour with Jesus (John iii. 22, iv. 2), but
this second summons was evidently a more definite and formal
'call' to discipleship[2]. See Luke v. 1–11.

[1] G. A. Smith, *Hist. Geog. of the Holy Land*, ch. xxii.
[2] Latham, *Pastor Pastorum*, 197, 198.

17 in the sea : for they were fishers. And Jesus said unto
them, Come ye after me, and I will make you to become
18 fishers of men. And straightway they left the nets, and
19 followed him. And going on a little further, he saw
James the *son* of Zebedee, and John his brother, who
20 also were in the boat mending the nets. And straightway
he called them : and they left their father Zebedee in the
boat with the hired servants, and went after him.

21   And they go into Capernaum ; and straightway on
the sabbath day he entered into the synagogue and
22 taught. And they were astonished at his teaching : for
he taught them as having authority, and not as the
23 scribes. And straightway there was in their synagogue

---

19. James...and John. Partners in the fishing industry with
Simon and Andrew (Luke v. 7, 10). Their mother was Salome.

21. Capernaum = ' village of Nahum,' probably on the N.W.
of the Lake[1]. For site, which is disputed, see Map. **synagogue**
(see Luke vii. 5). These buildings were used : (1) for the Sabbath
service, (2) as schools, (3) as courts of justice (cf. xiii. 9). The
service consisted of prayer, a Scripture lesson, and an exposition,
given by any competent Jew whom the 'ruler' called upon.

22. were astonished. Mark specially calls attention to the
effect of our Lord's words on the people and on the scribes.
he taught. Probably He expounded some passage of the
Jewish Scriptures (cf. Luke iv. 16), showing the *spirit* of the
Law, rather than its literal interpretation, instead of merely
quoting the usual traditional explanations of the Rabbinic com-
mentators. **the scribes.** A better title would be 'teachers of
the Law,' for they were the authorised expounders of the written
Law and its traditional explanations, and formed the learned
class of the nation. They taught elaborate and fanciful interpretations to the people, which tended to hamper their daily life
with minute and impossible rules of conduct[2]. See Matt. xv. 9,
xxiii. 2—36.

23. an unclean spirit. The man was apparently what we
should term 'a lunatic,' though the form of his insanity is not
easy to determine. The Jews believed that disease was the work
of evil spirits, and that lunatics and epileptics were 'possessed'
by demons, who spoke through the medium of their victims.

---

[1] G. A. Smith, *Hist. Geog. of the Holy Land,* 456 note.
[2] Robertson Smith, *The O.T. in the Jewish Church,* 42 foll. *Ecce Homo,*
ch. xxi. Moorhouse, *The Teaching of Christ,* Lect. IV.

a man with an unclean spirit; and he cried out, saying, 24
What have we to do with thee, thou Jesus of Nazareth?
art thou come to destroy us? I know thee who thou art,
the Holy One of God.   And Jesus rebuked him, saying, 25
Hold thy peace, and come out of him.   And the unclean 26
spirit, tearing him and crying with a loud voice, came
out of him.   And they were all amazed, insomuch that 27
they questioned among themselves, saying, What is this?
a new teaching! with authority he commandeth even the
unclean spirits, and they obey him.   And the report of 28
him went out straightway everywhere into all the region
of Galilee round about.

And straightway, when they were come out of the 29
synagogue, they came into the house of Simon and
Andrew, with James and John.   Now Simon's wife's 30
mother lay sick of a fever; and straightway they tell him
of her: and he came and took her by the hand, and 31
raised her up; and the fever left her, and she ministered
unto them.

And at even, when the sun did set, they brought unto 32

Our Lord evidently took the current beliefs on the subject as He
found them, just as He accepted the popular interpretations of
the O.T.[1]

24.   The lunatic cries out, 'What have we (evil spirits) in
common with thee?'   In some way he recognizes the power of
Jesus.   **the Holy One of God.**   A Messianic title, applied to
Jesus by Peter (John vi. 69).   It means literally 'the consecrated,'
i.e. to God, in this case.   Cf. Ps. xvi. 10, cvi. 16.

25.   **Hold thy peace,** lit. 'Be gagged.'   The same verb is used
in iv. 39, and Matt. xxii. 34.

26.   **tearing him,** R.V. Marg. 'convulsing,' a medical term.

30.   Peter's wife is mentioned by St Paul, see 1 Cor. ix. 5.

31.   **ministered unto them.**   Probably she served the mid-
day meal after the synagogue service.   The detail shows her
complete recovery.

32.   **at even.**   The Sabbath ended at sunset, and the people
were then free to bring their sick, without fear of 'breaking the
Sabbath.'

[1] Hastings' *Dict. of the Bible*, 'Jesus Christ.'

him all that were sick, and them that were possessed with
33 devils. And all the city was gathered together at the
34 door. And he healed many that were sick with divers
diseases, and cast out many devils ; and he suffered not
the devils to speak, because they knew him.

35 And in the morning, a great while before day, he rose
up and went out, and departed into a desert place,
36 and there prayed. And Simon and they that were with
37 him followed after him ; and they found him, and say
38 unto him, All are seeking thee. And he saith unto them,
Let us go elsewhere into the next towns, that I may
39 preach there also ; for to this end came I forth. And
he went into their synagogues throughout all Galilee,
preaching and casting out devils.

A. (*b*). 40-45. *First Preaching Tour in Synagogues of Galilee.*

40 And there cometh to him a leper, beseeching him, and

---

34. Jesus would not obtain notoriety through unworthy
channels. Cf. *v.* 25. R.V. Marg. adds to the words **they knew
Him** 'to be. Christ' ; see Luke iv. 41, whence the words are
probably copied.

35. a desert place. Probably a ravine leading down to the
Lake from the mountains. **and there prayed.** Cf. vi. 46,
xiv. 32; Luke vi. 12, ix. 18, 28, xi. 1, for instances of other
occasions when He felt the necessity of prayer for guidance.

38. the next towns. The Greek word used denotes small
country towns, of which there were many in Galilee.

preach. Note our Lord's own definition here of His work
and mission. **came I forth**, i.e. 'from the Father.' Cf.
John viii. 42, xiii. 3.

A. (*b*). 40-45. *First Preaching Tour in Synagogues of Galilee.*
[*Matt. iv.* 23, *viii.* 2-4. *Luke iv.* 42-44.]

39. This *v.* covers the work of several weeks, while 21-34
record the events of one Sabbath-day. Only one incident in
this tour is given in detail. It is described also by Matt. and
Luke, but in different contexts. Luke (iv. 44) says the tour
extended to Judaea also. Evidently insanity in some peculiar
form (see note on *v.* 23) was extraordinarily common in Palestine
at this time.

40. a leper. They were forbidden to enter a town, not

kneeling down to him, and saying unto him, If thou wilt, thou canst make me clean. And being moved with 41 compassion, he stretched forth his hand, and touched him, and saith unto him, I will; be thou made clean. And straightway the leprosy departed from him, and 42 he was made clean. And he strictly charged him, and 43 straightway sent him out, and saith unto him, See thou 44 say nothing to any man : but go thy way, shew thyself to the priest, and offer for thy cleansing the things which Moses commanded, for a testimony unto them. But he 45 went out, and began to publish it much, and to spread abroad the matter, insomuch that Jesus could no more

---

from fear of infection, but because leprosy was regarded by the Law as symbolical of sin, and those suffering from it were treated as moral outcasts. Jesus in curing and especially in *touching* this leper acted a parable, while He performed a miracle, for He showed forth His attitude towards sin[1].

41. touched him, thus breaking the Law, and showing thereby His disregard for its purely ceremonial side, when occasion demanded such a breach. **I will.** The patient's own faith was necessary to the cure, cf. vi. 5, 6; Matt. xiii. 58.

43. strictly, R.V. marg. 'sternly.' Jesus had no wish to attain cheap popularity as a wonder-worker, such as the people already looked for in their low and utterly mistaken conceptions of the Messiah. Also His work would have been hampered by large crowds in attendance, especially as their enthusiasm was likely to take some undesirable form, as on the occasion described in John vi. 15.

44. shew thyself. A reference to the careful rules for such a case given in Lev. xiii., xiv. Jesus here observed the Law, though He broke it where its regulations conflicted with the higher *spiritual* law, as in the case of Sabbath-observance (ii. 27, iii. 4) and ceremonial washings (vii. 2–8). Cf. also the incident of the half-shekel, Matt. xvii. 24–27[2]. **Moses**, the reputed author of the whole Pentateuch. Jesus, as always in such cases, accepts the ordinary belief.

a testimony unto them, i.e. the priests, who must be told of this new Power that they might then consider whether He might not be indeed the Messiah. The leper's disobedience put an end to the preaching tour amongst the synagogues.

---

[1] Plumptre on Matt. viii. 1–4. Edersheim, *Life*, I. 491 foll.
[2] Hort, *Judaistic Christianity*, 28–30.

openly enter into a city, but was without in desert places : and they came to him from every quarter.

A. (c). ii. 1–iii. 12.   *Second Visit to Capernaum.*

2 And when he entered again into Capernaum after 2 some days, it was noised that he was in the house. And many were gathered together, so that there was no longer room *for them*, no, not even about the door : and he 3 spake the word unto them. And they come, bringing 4 unto him a man sick of the palsy, borne of four. And when they could not come nigh unto him for the crowd, they uncovered the roof where he was : and when they had broken it up, they let down the bed whereon the sick 5 of the palsy lay. And Jesus seeing their faith saith unto 6 the sick of the palsy, Son, thy sins are forgiven. But there were certain of the scribes sitting there, and

---

A. (c). ii. 1–iii. 12.   *Second Visit to Capernaum.*
[*Matt. ix.* 1–17, *xii.* 1–21.   *Luke v.* 17–39, *vi.* 1–11.]

II.   1.   after some days, a quite vague interval of time.
in the house. R.V. marg. 'at home.' Possibly Simon's house: cf. i. 29–34.
2.   the word, here practically = 'the Gospel,' in which sense the Greek word was used at a later time: e.g. Acts viii. 4.
4.   uncovered the roof, i.e. took off some of the projecting wooden tiles and the pressed-down earth with which the roof would be covered. The description is not detailed enough to make quite clear the construction of the house[1]. The Gk word used for 'bed' here stands for a mat or goatskin rug.
5.   seeing their faith, see note on i. 41. Here the faith of the man's *friends* was sufficient.   **thy sins.** Jesus saw that the man's heart was heavy with a sense of sin (just as in *v.* 8 He read the scribes' thoughts). The Jews held that disease was a punishment for sin, so that the method used by Jesus would appeal at once to the patient[2]. Jesus claims him by using the title 'son' (lit. 'child'), the word used elsewhere of disciples.
6.   Luke explains that scribes had come from Jerusalem to watch Jesus. No doubt they had come across Him at Jerusalem (see John ii. 23) the year before.

[1] See Edersheim, *Life*, I. 501 foll.
[2] *Id. ibid.* I. 507 foll. (Rabbinical teaching on sin and forgiveness).

reasoning in their hearts, Why doth this man thus speak? 7
he blasphemeth: who can forgive sins but one, *even* God?
And straightway Jesus, perceiving in his spirit that they 8
so reasoned within themselves, saith unto them, Why
reason ye these things in your hearts? Whether is easier, 9
to say to the sick of the palsy, Thy sins are forgiven; or
to say, Arise, and take up thy bed, and walk? But that 10
ye may know that the Son of man hath power on earth to
forgive sins (he saith to the sick of the palsy), I say unto 11
thee, Arise, take up thy bed, and go unto thy house.
And he arose, and straightway took up the bed, and 12
went forth before them all; insomuch that they were
all amazed, and glorified God, saying, We never saw
it on this fashion.

---

7. he blasphemeth. A sin which was punished by death—
see xiv. 63, 64 and 1 Kings xxi. 13.

8. perceiving in his spirit. See n. on *v.* 5, and cf. John
ii. 24, 25.

9. The scribes would at once feel that it was an easier thing
to proclaim forgiveness (of which there could be no outward
proof) than to command 'with power' a cripple to use his
limbs, since there would be immediate proof of the efficacy
(or the reverse) of such words. But Jesus had a deeper meaning
in His questions. Only One who was Divine could forgive sins,
but such an One could also perform the *lesser* miracle of healing
the sinner's body.

10. the Son of man. Jesus applies this title frequently to
Himself, 14 times in this Gospel alone. It is not certain if
it is based on Dan. vii. 13. The phrase means 'the Representative Man,' One who is Man in a special sense, the 'Ideal
Man.' Cf. the phrases 'son of peace,' 'son of Belial' (='worth-
lessness')[1].

power. R.V. marg. 'authority,' i.e. the Divine commission.

11. Arise, take up thy bed. The same words He had
addressed to the cripple at Bethesda (John v. 8), in both
cases requiring faith on the part of the sufferer. See n. on
i. 41.

12. This miracle was as public as possible, perhaps because
Jesus wished His claim to *forgive sins* to be made known, which
was the moral purpose of the cure.

[1] Westcott on St John's Gospel, pp. 33 foll.

13 And he went forth again by the sea side ; and all the
14 multitude resorted unto him, and he taught them. And
as he passed by, he saw Levi the *son* of Alphæus sitting
at the place of toll, and he saith unto him, Follow me.
15 And he arose and followed him. And it came to pass,
that he was sitting at meat in his house, and many
publicans and sinners sat down with Jesus and his
disciples : for there were many, and they followed him.
16 And the scribes of the Pharisees, when they saw that

13–III. 6. Further encounters of Jesus with the Pharisees,
probably placed here on account of the similarity of subject.

14. Levi, generally identified with Matthew ; see Matt. ix. 9.
Possibly the name Matthew (= 'gift of God') was given him
after his call, as Simon was re-named Peter (Cephas).

Alphæus, probably a different person from the father of
'James the Less,' iii. 18.

the place of toll, situated on the high-road which ran from
Damascus to the Mediterranean coast, and thence to Phoenicia.
The Roman taxes were farmed by Roman capitalists, and the
collectors (called in the N.T. 'publicans') made what profit they
could in the process of collecting, and were often cruel and
extortionate officials.

Follow me. Levi's obedience meant the total loss of his
means of livelihood. He could not, like the fishermen, resume
his post.

15. sitting at meat. The verb implies the posture of reclining
on the elbow, the usual Oriental position at meals.

his house, i.e. Levi's, who was evidently giving his friends a
farewell feast.

sinners probably indicates any who were not strict Jews, and
also men of Gentile extraction. The word would be so used by
the scribes.

16. the scribes of the Pharisees (cf. Acts xxiii. 9), the scribes
of the Pharisee sect, probably the deputation from Jerusalem,
ii. 6. The sect arose in the time of the Maccabee revolt against
Syrian oppression, and kept alive in the nation religious fervour
and patriotic zeal. In our Lord's time they represented extreme
Jewish ideas in politics and religion, as opposed to the lax views
of the Sadducee priesthood, and they had become at that period
punctilious in observing the minutiae of the Law, while they
regarded the Roman government with hatred as an outrage on
the independence of the sacred nation. Their name means
'separatists.'

he was eating with the sinners and publicans, said unto his disciples, He eateth and drinketh with publicans and sinners. And when Jesus heard it, he saith unto them, 17 They that are whole have no need of a physician, but they that are sick : I came not to call the righteous, but sinners.

And John's disciples and the Pharisees were fasting : 18 and they come and say unto him, Why do John's disciples and the disciples of the Pharisees fast, but thy disciples fast not? And Jesus said unto them, Can the sons of the 19 bride-chamber fast, while the bridegroom is with them? as long as they have the bridegroom with them, they cannot fast. But the days will come, when the bridegroom 20

Eating with Gentiles or sinners was regarded as lax conduct by the stricter Jews : cf. the restrictions of caste among Hindus. See Gal. ii. 12.

17. They that are whole, etc. A proverb familiar to His hearers.

the righteous, i.e. those who consider themselves perfect, and in no need of salvation, the 'self-righteous,' as we say now. Matthew adds here our Lord's counsel to the Pharisees to study the teaching of the prophets about formal religion, "I will have mercy and not sacrifice."

18. were fasting. From the time of the Captivity onwards the practice of fasting among the Jews was much developed, and in our Lord's time strict observers of the traditional law fasted twice a week, on the 2nd and 5th day (cf. Luke xviii. 12, "I fast twice in the week"). The Day of Atonement had been originally the only fast-day in the year. John's disciples naturally followed the practice of their ascetic master.

19. sons of the bride-chamber, the groomsmen, or personal friends of the bridegroom : cf. Judges xiv. 11. Possibly the feast in Levi's house suggested the thought of a wedding-festivity. The 'groomsmen' were exempt from certain religious observances, including the fasts, during the time of a wedding-festival.

20. the bridegroom. Jesus here claims a Messianic title, see Is. liv. 1–10 (cf. Rev. xix. 7). The 'bride' is that part of mankind which He chooses, the wedding is His mystical union with mankind, which His disciples were celebrating with joy as long as He remained with them. Jesus therefore claims for

shall be taken away from them, and then will they fast in
21 that day. No man seweth a piece of undressed cloth
on an old garment : else that which should fill it up
taketh from it, the new from the old, and a worse rent is
22 made. And no man putteth new wine into old wine-
skins : else the wine will burst the skins, and the wine
perisheth, and the skins : but *they put* new wine into
fresh wine-skins.

23   And it came to pass, that he was going on the
sabbath day through the cornfields ; and his disciples
24 began, as they went, to pluck the ears of corn. And the
Pharisees said unto him, Behold, why do they on the
25 sabbath day that which is not lawful ? And he said unto

His disciples the groomsmen's privilege of exemption from
Jewish tradition[1].

then will they fast. A prediction, not a command.

22. wine-skins. See R.V. marg. 'skins used as bottles.' If
old skins already soaked in wine were used, they would cause
too violent fermentation, and so would burst. The connexion
of these two parables with the teaching of the preceding verses
is not at first obvious. Our Lord in 19, 20, justifies His disciples
in not fasting as tradition requires; in 21, 22, He justifies John's
disciples in fasting according to that tradition[2]. The latter
belonged to the 'old' order, and could not with profit 'tack on'
to it fragments of the 'new.' The Christian principles and the
Christian spirit must be imparted *gradually* ; the Gospel does
not destroy the Law, it fulfils and amplifies it, breathing into
it new life and spirit. Cf. the teaching in the Sermon on the
Mount on this subject, and St Paul's words in Rom. xiv.

24. the Pharisees, probably once more the Jerusalem deputation, who may have been present on the occasion of the former
Sabbath miracles. John v. 10–16.

that which is not lawful. The Law (Deut. xxiii. 25) allowed
the wayfarer to pluck corn, but the rigorous Pharisee would
regard this as reaping, and reaping is *work*, which was forbidden
on the Sabbath[3]. Such literalness seems to us childish and absurd,
but the traditions of the scribes upheld it strongly as 'righteousness': cf. Luke vi. 1.

25. Jesus appealed to Scripture because the Rabbis them-

[1] Hort, *Judaistic Christianity*, 23.
[2] *Id. ibid.* 24.
[3] Edersheim, *Life*, Appendix XVII.

them, Did ye never read what David did, when he
had need, and was an hungred, he, and they that were
with him? How he entered into the house of God when 26
Abiathar was high priest, and did eat the shewbread,
which it is not lawful to eat save for the priests, and gave
also to them that were with him? And he said unto 27
them, The sabbath was made for man, and not man for
the sabbath: so that the Son of man is lord even of the 28
sabbath.

And he entered again into the synagogue; and there 3
was a man there which had his hand withered. And 2
they watched him, whether he would heal him on the
sabbath day; that they might accuse him. And he 3

---

selves constantly made such appeals in support of their position.
His reference was to show that even in their own Scriptures the
ceremonial law yielded on occasion to a law of humanity.

26. the house of God, i.e. the Tabernacle at Nob, 1 Sam.
xxi. 1–6.

when Abiathar was high priest. 1 Sam. places the incident
in the days of Ahimelech, father of Abiathar. The words,
being peculiar to Mark, may be a note of the writer's own, or
our Lord Himself may have made the slip, which is only
equivalent to a mistake in a date and does not affect His
argument. In taking our human nature upon Him He was
not (so far as we know) exempt from the ordinary weaknesses of
human memory.

the shewbread, lit. 'the loaves of showing,' i.e. the loaves
placed every Sabbath on the table before the veil, and afterwards eaten by the priests. See Lev. xxiv. 5–9.

27, 28. The principle was not unknown to the Rabbis; one
of them had even said "The Sabbath is handed over to you;
not, ye are handed over to the Sabbath." Jesus goes further,
declaring that He, the Son of Man, has authority over the
Sabbath, thus plainly showing forth His Divine commission.

27. This precept applied to the Christian Sunday would
suggest that its use, like that of any other gift of God, is to
be regulated by the requirements of God's service.

28. the Son of man, n. on 10. Here as 'Representative
of mankind' He claims to regulate the institution which was
God's gift to mankind.

is lord of, 'has the disposal of.'

III. 1. again, i.e. on another occasion.

2. heal him on the sabbath day. The Rabbis allowed

saith unto the man that had his hand withered, Stand
4 forth. And he saith unto them, Is it lawful on the
sabbath day to do good, or to do harm? to save a life,
5 or to kill? But they held their peace. And when he had
looked round about on them with anger, being grieved at
the hardening of their heart, he saith unto the man,
Stretch forth thy hand. And he stretched it forth:
6 and his hand was restored. And the Pharisees went
out, and straightway with the Herodians took counsel
against him, how they might destroy him.

7 And Jesus with his disciples withdrew to the sea: and
a great multitude from Galilee followed: and from Judæa,
8 and from Jerusalem, and from Idumæa, and beyond

---

healing on the Sabbath only if the patient's life was in danger[1].
Notice here the recognition of His *power* to heal.

4. to kill. Because to suffer curable disease to continue
means allowing Death to have its way[2]. Once more Jesus
points out that the law of mercy is higher than that of ceremonial
observance (note on ii. 25). The Rabbis were silent, feeling self-
condemned.

5. with anger, being grieved. Two human emotions, but
the first is divinely tempered by the second.

hardening = 'callousness,' the hardness as of a bony substance,
insensitive and resisting: cf. viii. 17, where it is used of the
disciples.

he stretched it forth, a proof of the man's faith. See
n. on i. 41.

6. the Herodians, i.e. those who sided with Herod, Jews
probably who saw in the rule of the Herods their only hope of
survival as a nation. The Pharisees hated the Roman rule,
but would make common cause with its supporters against a
common foe, as they would regard the new Teacher. The
Herodians appear again in viii. 15 and xii. 13, but nowhere
else.

7–12. Matthew (xii. 15–21) places this section after the
Mission of the Twelve.

8. Idumæa, the ancient Edom, but since the time of the
Maccabees practically a part of Palestine. The Herods were
Idumaeans. Aretas, father-in-law of Herod Antipas, was at this
time the ruler of Idumaea[3].

[1] Edersheim, *Life*, II. 59, 60.
[2] See Hort, *The Way, the Truth, the Life*, 102, 103.
[3] G. A. Smith, *Hist. Geog. of the Holy Land*, 240.

Jordan, and about Tyre and Sidon, a great multitude, hearing what great things he did, came unto him. And he spake to his disciples, that a little boat should wait on him because of the crowd, lest they should throng him : for he had healed many ; insomuch that as many as had plagues pressed upon him that they might touch him. And the unclean spirits, whensoever they beheld him, fell down before him, and cried, saying, Thou art the Son of God. And he charged them much that they should not make him known. 9 10 11 12

SECOND SECTION. [iii. 13–vi. 6 *a*.]

B. (*a*). *Call of the Twelve.*

And he goeth up into the mountain, and calleth unto him whom he himself would : and they went unto him. And he appointed twelve, that they might be with him, 13 14

----

beyond Jordan, i.e. the district called Peraea, visited by Jesus at the end of the Galilean ministry (x. 1).

12. that they should not make him known. The time had not yet come for a general declaration of His Messiahship, and He would not accept the testimony of demoniacs.

B. (*a*). *Call of the Twelve.*
[*Matt. x.* 2–4. *Luke vi.* 12–19.]

13. the mountain, i.e. the hill country on the west of the Lake. From St Luke (vi. 12) we learn that He spent the whole night in prayer.

14. appointed twelve. First He invited a number of followers to come to Him ('calleth unto him'), and then chose out Twelve of these ('he appointed twelve') for a special purpose. **twelve.** Possibly the number was suggested by the number of the Tribes, the old Israel, now to be succeeded by the new Christian community. Cf. also Matt. xix. 28, Rev. xxi. 14. The Westcott-Hort Gk text inserts after 'twelve' the words 'whom also he named apostles' (see Luke vi. 13). The word translated 'apostles' (lit. ' sent forth ') means in classical Greek 'envoys': here therefore the name implies that the chosen Twelve were the envoys of the Heavenly King, sent out to do His work. Details of their later 'mission' are given in vi. 7. In the Gospel narrative they are usually called 'the Twelve,' or 'the disciples' (lit. 'learners'), for it was their chief work to 'learn' till after the Resurrection[1].

[1] Hort, *The Christian Ecclesia*, Lect. II.

15 and that he might send them forth to preach, and to have
16 authority to cast out devils: and Simon he surnamed
17 Peter; and James the *son* of Zebedee, and John the
brother of James; and them he surnamed Boanerges,
18 which is, Sons of thunder: and Andrew, and Philip, and
Bartholomew, and Matthew, and Thomas, and James the

---

15. Their work (as His representatives) was identical with that of Jesus Himself on His recent tour, "preaching and casting out devils," i. 39.

The discourse called the Sermon on the Mount was apparently (in part at least) given now as an instruction to the Twelve and the other 'learners.'

16.   surnamed Peter, i.e. on a previous occasion, see John i. 42. The new name (= 'Rock') is fully explained in Matt. xvi. 18. These first three disciples (all re-named by our Lord) were with Him at the Transfiguration, the healing of Jairus' daughter, and the Agony in the Garden.

17.   Boanerges. The derivation of this word is unknown. **sons of thunder,** i.e. men of impetuous character, as is shown by the incidents recorded in ix. 38; Luke ix. 54; Matt. xx. 21. See also John's fiery language in 1 John ii. 4, iii. 8, etc.

18.   Andrew, and Philip, Greek names like Simon's. All three were from Bethsaida, a centre of Greek influence. **Bartholomew** (= 'son of Tolmai': cf. Bar-Jesus, Bar-nabas, etc.). He is generally identified with Nathanael, who was a native of Cana. See John i. 46.

Matthew, generally identified with Levi: ii. 14.

Thomas, also called 'the Twin' or Didymus: John xi. 16.

James the son of Alphæus, so called to distinguish him from the son of Zebedee. He is usually identified with James 'the Little' (xv. 40), but is not the same as James 'the brother of the Lord,' the writer of the Epistle and a man of high position in the Church at Jerusalem. Levi's father was also called Alphaeus (ii. 14), but the name was probably not uncommon.

Thaddæus. Luke calls him Judas: cf. also John xiv. 22. He is not the same as Jude, 'the brother of the Lord,' and writer of the Epistle. Another Gk MS. gives his name here as Lebbaeus. The two names imply courage (Lebbaeus) and gentleness (Thaddaeus).

the Cananæan = 'Zealot,' the name of a fanatical party amongst the Jews, often distinguished for their violence and sedition. Possibly the name is here applied only to Simon's personal character, as a man very 'zealous' for the right.

son of Alphæus, and Thaddæus, and Simon the Cananæan, 19
and Judas Iscariot, which also betrayed him.

B. (b). *Third visit to Capernaum.*

And he cometh into a house. And the multitude 20
cometh together again, so that they could not so much
as eat bread. And when his friends heard it, they went 21
out to lay hold on him : for they said, He is beside
himself. And the scribes which came down from Jeru- 22
salem said, He hath Beelzebub, and, By the prince of
the devils casteth he out the devils. And he called them 23

---

19. Iscariot = a native of Kerioth, a small town either in
Judaea or E. of the Dead Sea. He was the only one of the
Twelve who was not a Galilean. He is rarely named in the
Gospels without mention of his treachery.
There are four lists of the Apostles, one in each of the first
three Gospels and one in Acts i. 13 : no two agree exactly, but
in each the names fall into three groups of four each, and in
each Peter, Philip, and James son of Alphaeus head the three
groups.

B. (b). *Third Visit to Capernaum.*
[*Matt. ix.* 32–34, *xii.* 46–40. *Luke viii.* 19–21.]

Between the two clauses of *v.* 19 we should place the Sermon
on the Mount and the return to Capernaum.
The 'house' into which He entered was probably Peter's.
21. his friends, i.e. either His family or disciples, or both.
This *v.* (21) anticipates what occurs later, in *v.* 31.
22. the scribes...from Jerusalem. A deputation sent down
to watch the new Teacher : cf. ii. 16. Their accusation was
apparently called forth by the cure of a blind and dumb demoniac
(Matt. xii. 22).
Beelzebub. Apparently the name of a heathen god, and
applied derisively to the Evil One from the belief that the 'gods'
of the heathen were evil spirits. Jesus was charged again at
Jerusalem (John vii. 20) with using 'magic' to effect His cures.
23. Jesus answered the charge of His being a *ruler* over
evil spirits by proving that He was their *enemy*, and therefore
it was absurd to accuse Him of being in league with their
prince.
in parables, i.e. in 'proverbs' or 'dark sayings'; lit. 'in
comparisons.' The 'illustrative story' is a third meaning of the
word, not intended here.

unto him, and said unto them in parables, How can Satan
24 cast out Satan? And if a kingdom be divided against
25 itself, that kingdom cannot stand. And if a house be
divided against itself, that house will not be able to stand.
26 And if Satan hath risen up against himself, and is divided,
27 he cannot stand, but hath an end. But no one can enter
into the house of the strong *man*, and spoil his goods,
except he first bind the strong *man*; and then he will
28 spoil his house. Verily I say unto you, All their sins
shall be forgiven unto the sons of men, and their blasphe-
29 mies wherewith soever they shall blaspheme : but whosoever shall blaspheme against the Holy Spirit hath never
30 forgiveness, but is guilty of an eternal sin : because they
said, He hath an unclean spirit.
31   And there come his mother and his brethren ; and,

Satan, lit. 'the adversary': see i. 13.

24–26. The 'proverbs' of the Divided Kingdom and the
Divided House are *illustrations* of the argument used by Jesus.

27. As usual (cf. ii. 27, 28, iii. 4) Jesus, having answered
His adversaries' objection, now goes on to expound His own
teaching.

the strong man, i.e. Satan, whom only God can conquer.
Jesus therefore claims here Divine power (cf. ii. 10).

28. Verily I say unto you. The usual prelude to a specially
solemn saying of our Lord's.

29, 30. The scribes had uttered terrible blasphemy in identifying with the spirit of evil the Holy Spirit of God, by whom
Jesus cast out the demons.

29. is guilty of, lit. 'is still bound by.'

an eternal sin, 'a sin which goes on into the next life,'
i.e. which cannot be forgiven in this life. Forgiveness can
only come through the Spirit whom the scribes by their very
words denied.

30. because they said, etc. A note by the writer to explain
why such solemn warning had been uttered: see also Luke xii. 10.

31–35. Luke (viii. 19–21) places this incident *after* the
teaching by parables.

31. his brethren, James, Joses, Judas, and Simon (vi. 3).
Either they were sons of Joseph by a former marriage, and so by
repute half-brothers to our Lord, or they were His own younger

standing without, they sent unto him, calling him. And 32
a multitude was sitting about him; and they say unto
him, Behold, thy mother and thy brethren without seek
for thee. And he answereth them, and saith, Who is my 33
mother and my brethren? And looking round on them 34
which sat round about him, he saith, Behold, my mother
and my brethren! For whosoever shall do the will of 35
God, the same is my brother, and sister, and mother.

B. (c). Teaching by the Lake side: Group of Parables.

And again he began to teach by the sea side. And **4**
there is gathered unto him a very great multitude, so that
he entered into a boat, and sat in the sea; and all the
multitude were by the sea on the land. And he taught 2
them many things in parables, and said unto them in his
teaching, Hearken: Behold, the sower went forth to sow: 3

---

brothers, children of Mary and Joseph[1]. Mary does not appear
again in this Gospel.

35. Compare our Lord's teaching here with His words in
x. 29. Even natural affection must yield to a higher call: but
Jesus to the end thought tenderly for His mother (John xix. 26,
27), and some of His brothers came to believe on Him (see n. on
18, and Acts i. 14).

B. (c). Teaching by the Lake side: Group of Parables.

[*Matt. xiii.* 1–53. *Luke viii.* 4–18.]

IV. A new stage in Jesus' teaching begins here with the first
recorded 'parable,' or illustrative story[2]. Till now He has
preached repentance, the coming of a new Kingdom, its laws,
and His own authority. He now begins to explain what 'the
Kingdom' means.

2. in parables (see n. on iii. 23). His imagery is often taken
from something visible at the moment. Probably His audience
could see a man sowing a cornfield on the slopes which ran down
to the Lake.

3. Hearken. He arrests attention at the beginning and close
of the parable (*v.* 9).

[1] Lightfoot's *Galatians*, 'The Brethren of the Lord.'
[2] On the Parables generally, see Trench, *On the Parables*; Bruce, *The Parabolic Teaching of Christ*; Hastings' *Dict. of the Bible*, 'Parables.'

4 and it came to pass, as he sowed, some *seed* fell by the
5 way side, and the birds came and devoured it. And other
fell on the rocky *ground*, where it had not much earth;
and straightway it sprang up, because it had no deepness
6 of earth : and when the sun was risen, it was scorched ;
7 and because it had no root, it withered away. And other
fell among the thorns, and the thorns grew up, and choked
8 it, and it yielded no fruit. And others fell into the good
ground, and yielded fruit, growing up and increasing ;
and brought forth, thirtyfold, and sixtyfold, and a hundred-
9 fold. And he said, Who hath ears to hear, let him hear.
10 And when he was alone, they that were about him
11 with the twelve asked of him the parables. And he said
unto them, Unto you is given the mystery of the kingdom
of God : but unto them that are without, all things are

---

4. the way side, the trodden pathway dividing one field from another.

7. the thorns, i.e. the unweeded part of the field, overgrown with *thistles* and other thorny weeds which are specially prevalent in Palestine.

8. a hundredfold. Not an unheard-of crop in the fertile parts of Palestine[1]. Note that three degrees of fruitfulness correspond to the three degrees of unfruitfulness.

9. Who hath ears to hear, etc. The formula occurs six times in the first three Gospels and often in the Book of the Revelation : possibly it was used by the Rabbis. Jesus always meant His hearers to ponder on His words, and so He spoke in parables and paradoxes, which they would be likely to remember afterwards[2].

11. the mystery. The Gk word was used for a secret form of worship, revealed only to the initiated. Here probably it means an 'inner teaching reserved only for a chosen few,' i.e. for the disciples, who were however to tell it out in later days to those whom they in turn instructed.

the kingdom of God, called often in Matthew 'the Kingdom of heaven.'

them that are without, i.e. those to whom the 'mystery' is not yet revealed : the Rabbis used the phrase to describe Gentiles or lax Jews : cf. 1 Cor. v. 12.

[1] Merrill, *Galilee*, ch. v.
[2] Latham, *Pastor Pastorum*, ch. x.

done in parables : that seeing they may see, and not 12
perceive ; and hearing they may hear, and not understand ; lest haply they should turn again, and it should
be forgiven them.   And he saith unto them, Know ye not 13
this parable ? and how shall ye know all the parables ?
The sower soweth the word.   And these are they by the ¹⁴
way side, where the word is sown ; and when they have ₁₅
heard, straightway cometh Satan, and taketh away the
word which hath been sown in them.   And these in like 16
manner are they that are sown upon the rocky *places*,
who, when they have heard the word, straightway receive
it with joy ; and they have no root in themselves, but 17
endure for a while ; then, when tribulation or persecution
ariseth because of the word, straightway they stumble.
And others are they that are sown among the thorns ; 18
these are they that have heard the word, and the cares 19

---

12. that seeing they may see, etc.   The words are adapted
from Is. vi. 9, 10, and are part of the prophet's commission.
The preacher's *expectation* of inattentive hearers is of course
an ironical way of describing the case, for neither Isaiah nor
Jesus *intended* that their preaching should wholly fail.

14–20. The following points are left unexplained.   (1) The
identity of the Sower, who stands apparently for the agency
by which 'the word' is made known, including its preaching
through Christ and His Church[1].   (2) The meaning of the
various kinds of soil, for these are *not* the hearers, who are
signified by the 'seed,' developed variously according to the
soil.   Note also that the interpretation of the parable is con-
fused with its imagery : e.g. 'those who are sown...are they
who...' etc.

17. they stumble, lit. 'are made to stumble,' the old Eng.
sense of 'to offend.'

The four classes of hearers may be thus briefly summarized :

(1) the spiritually dull, in whom the word produces no result,
(2) the thoughtlessly impulsive, in whom it produces no lasting
result,
(3) the half-hearted, who give to it only a part of their
attention,
(4) the whole-hearted, to whom it is all in all [2].

---

[1] Hort, *Village Sermons*, 57 foll.
[2] Bruce, *The Parabolic Teaching of Christ*, ch. I.

of the world, and the deceitfulness of riches, and the lusts
of other things entering in, choke the word, and it be-
20 cometh unfruitful. And those are they that were sown
upon the good ground : such as hear the word, and accept
it, and bear fruit, thirtyfold, and sixtyfold, and a hundredfold.

21 And he said unto them, Is the lamp brought to be put
under the bushel, or under the bed, *and* not to be put on
22 the stand? For there is nothing hid, save that it should
be manifested ; neither was *anything* made secret, but
23 that it should come to light. If any man hath ears to
24 hear, let him hear. And he said unto them, Take heed
what ye hear : with what measure ye mete it shall be
measured unto you : and more shall be given unto you.
25 For he that hath, to him shall be given : and he that hath
not, from him shall be taken away even that which he
hath.

26 And he said, So is the kingdom of God, as if a man
27 should cast seed upon the earth ; and should sleep and

21, 22. This passage is an appendix to the interpretation of
'The Sower,' after which in Matt. xiii. several other parables
are added. The parable of the Lamp was to show that the
Master's teaching ('the lamp') though at first revealed only to
the disciples ('the lamp-stand'), was to be by them made known
to the world.

23. If any man hath ears, cf. *v.* 9.

24, 25. Two more proverbial sayings, possibly already familiar
to His hearers. They occur again in a different context Matt. v. 15,
vii. 2, x. 26; Luke vi. 38, xi. 33, xii. 2, xix. 26[1].

24. The meaning is 'Attend well, since you will yourself
profit by the teaching which you impart to others, in proportion
to the attention you give to it.'

25. This saying cannot refer to the possession of material
things. It means here 'The more capacity you have for
learning, the more it will be imparted to you: but if you are
unable to learn, you will go backward instead of forward.'

26—29. This parable is the only one recorded by Mark alone.

26. From this point Jesus appears to be addressing the people
generally.

[1] Latham, *Pastor Pastorum*, ch. **x.**

rise night and day, and the seed should spring up and grow, he knoweth not how. The earth beareth fruit of 28 herself; first the blade, then the ear, then the full corn in the ear. But when the fruit is ripe, straightway he putteth 29 forth the sickle, because the harvest is come.

And he said, How shall we liken the kingdom of God? 30 or in what parable shall we set it forth? It is like a 31 grain of mustard seed, which, when it is sown upon the earth, though it be less than all the seeds that are upon the earth, yet when it is sown, groweth up, and becometh 32 greater than all the herbs, and putteth out great branches; so that the birds of the heaven can lodge under the shadow thereof.

And with many such parables spake he the word unto 33 them, as they were able to hear it : and without a parable 34 spake he not unto them : but privately to his own disciples he expounded all things.

---

28. **of herself**, i.e. without man's agency.

29. Most of the verse is quoted from Joel iii. 13. Jewish teachers often made use in this way of O.T. language.

Christ is 'the man' who sows the field of the Kingdom of God, and will reap it hereafter; meanwhile it grows mysteriously.

31. **mustard.** There is a variety which in the Jordan valley grows into a tree-like plant. 'Small as mustard-seed' was a common comparison among the Jews.

32. **the birds of the heaven**, etc.: cf. Dan. iv. 12 and Ezek. xvii. 22–24. The rapid growth of the Kingdom was shown by the spread of the Gospel, at first entrusted to a little band of disciples, and then reaching forth throughout the Roman Empire. These three parables are all connected by the idea of the growth of seed, and the lesson that the *ground*, i.e. the human spirit, is all important, is found in all three. Luke gives the 'mustard-seed' parable in a different context (Luke xiii. 18, 19); possibly Jesus repeated His parables.

33. **many such parables.** Matthew (xiii.) gives five more in this place.

B. (d). *Expedition to East side of the Lake.*

35 And on that day, when even was come, he saith unto
36 them, Let us go over unto the other side. And leaving
the multitude, they take him with them, even as he was,
37 in the boat. And other boats were with him. And there
ariseth a great storm of wind, and the waves beat into
38 the boat, insomuch that the boat was now filling. And he
himself was in the stern, asleep on the cushion : and they
awake him, and say unto him, Master, carest thou not
39 that we perish? And he awoke, and rebuked the wind,
and said unto the sea, Peace, be still. And the wind
40 ceased, and there was a great calm. And he said unto
41 them, Why are ye fearful? have ye not yet faith? And
they feared exceedingly, and said one to another, Who
then is this, that even the wind and the sea obey him?

B. (d). *Expedition to East side of the Lake.*
[*Matt. viii.* 13-34. *Luke viii.* 23-39.]

36. Matt. (viii. 18-22) here inserts the account of two men
who wished to follow Jesus.

other boats. Probably they returned on the approach of the
storm.

37. a great storm. Sudden squalls frequently come down
from the ravines on the W. side of the Lake[1].

38. asleep. This is the only place where Our Lord is
mentioned as sleeping, though it is implied in other passages
(where He is stated, as something exceptional, to have been up all
night).

39. rebuked the wind, in the dramatic Oriental manner,
addressing wind and waves directly: cf. xi. 14, 23. See also
Ps. cvii. 29.

40. have ye not yet faith? i.e. 'after all that you have
learnt.'

41. feared exceedingly. This was the terror of great awe.

even the wind, etc., lit. 'the wind also,' i.e. as well as the
unclean spirits, to the fisherfolk a greater marvel than mastery
over demons. The miracle was also a 'parable' of the calming
effect of the Master's presence in all times of trouble, and again,
it prepared the disciples for belief in His power over the forces

[1] G. A. Smith, *Hist. Geog. of the Holy Land*, 441 foll.

And they came to the other side of the sea, into the 5
country of the Gerasenes. And when he was come out 2
of the boat, straightway there met him out of the tombs
a man with an unclean spirit, who had his dwelling in the 3
tombs : and no man could any more bind him, no, not
with a chain ; because that he had been often bound with 4
fetters and chains, and the chains had been rent asunder
by him, and the fetters broken in pieces : and no man
had strength to tame him. And always, night and day, 5
in the tombs and in the mountains, he was crying out,
and cutting himself with stones. And when he saw Jesus 6
from afar, he ran and worshipped him ; and crying out 7
with a loud voice, he saith, What have I to do with thee,
Jesus, thou Son of the Most High God? I adjure thee
by God, torment me not. For he said unto him, Come 8
forth, thou unclean spirit, out of the man. And he asked 9

---

of nature, which reached its climax in His victory over death.
Such 'preparation' was part of Jesus' plan of teaching[1].

V. 1. the other side. The character of the two districts is
quite different[2].

Gerasenes. In Matt. we find 'Gadarenes.' There was a
well-known town of Gerasa, but it was 30 miles from the Lake,
while Gadara was a place 6 miles away. (See Map.) Probably the
latter name covered at this time a whole *district*, and the incident
may have occurred near some small place within it, called
Gerasa, bordering on the Lake. There is a place with ancient
tombs and a steep slope on the E. shore which answers to the
description[3].

2. a man. Matt. mentions two. His account is less detailed
throughout than Mark's.

3. the tombs. Rock-caves, probably used for tombs, have
been found in the district. No sane Jew would enter a tomb,
since by doing so he incurred pollution.

4. Maniacs often display extraordinary muscular strength.

7. Most High God. The phrase was used by Gentiles as well
as Jews, and specially as a formula for 'exorcising' evil spirits ;
and may thus have become familiar to this demoniac. See n.
on i. 24, and cf. Acts xvi. 17.

[1] Latham, *Pastor Pastorum*, 88, 94.
[2] G. A. Smith, *Hist. Geog. of the Holy Land*, ch. xxviii. Hastings' *Dict.
of the Bible*, 'Decapolis.'
[3] Hastings' *Dict. of the Bible*, 'Gadara,' etc.

him, What is thy name? And he saith unto him, My
10 name is Legion; for we are many. And he besought
him much that he would not send them away out of the
11 country. Now there was there on the mountain side a
12 great herd of swine feeding. And they besought him,
saying, Send us into the swine, that we may enter into
13 them. And he gave them leave. And the unclean spirits
came out, and entered into the swine : and the herd
rushed down the steep into the sea, *in number* about two
14 thousand ; and they were choked in the sea. And they
that fed them fled, and told it in the city, and in the
country. And they came to see what it was that had
15 come to pass. And they come to Jesus, and behold him
that was possessed with devils sitting, clothed and in

---

9. What is thy name? Jesus showed special interest in
the man, and later commissioned him to preach to his own
people. (*v.* 19.)

Legion. A Latin word meaning a Roman regiment, whose
full number was nominally 6000. The man felt possessed by
countless devils[1].

10. out of the country. This was the man's own petition,
viz. that he might dwell still in his own land. The plural pro-
noun may be disregarded, as the man speaks now in his own
person (singular), now as a host of demons (plural).

12. swine. The owners cannot have been strict Jews, as it
was unlawful to keep swine.

13. were choked. Here (as in the withering of the Fig-tree
xi. 20) our Lord worked a miracle of destruction, evidently to
teach some specially important lesson, probably that of the power
of evil, of the 'strong man armed,' whom He, 'the stronger
man' (iii. 27), was able to control. This startling incident,
occurring *after* the man had become sane, would make a lasting
impression upon him, as well as upon the bystanders, and would
inspire him in the work of preaching, which was immediately
given him to do (18–20).

14. the city, probably Gerasa (n. on *v.* 1).

15. sitting. Luke adds 'at his feet,' i.e. in the attitude of a
disciple.

clothed. The Gk word implies 'in an upper garment' (or
himation).

[1] On Demoniac Possession, see Plumptre on St Matthew (Excursus);
Moorhouse, *The Teaching of Christ*; Hastings' *Dict. of the Bible*, 'Jesus
Christ.'

his right mind, *even* him that had the legion : and they
were afraid.   And they that saw it declared unto them 16
how it befell him that was possessed with devils, and
concerning the swine.   And they began to beseech him 17
to depart from their borders.   And as he was entering 18
into the boat, he that had been possessed with devils
besought him that he might be with him.   And he 19
suffered him not, but saith unto him, Go to thy house
unto thy friends, and tell them how great things the Lord
hath done for thee, and *how* he had mercy on thee.   And 20
he went his way, and began to publish in Decapolis how
great things Jesus had done for him : and all men did
marvel.

    B.   (e).   Return to West side of the Lake.

And when Jesus had crossed over again in the boat 21
unto the other side, a great multitude was gathered unto
him : and he was by the sea.   And there cometh one of 22
the rulers of the synagogue, Jaïrus by name ; and seeing

---

afraid.   Evidently terrified by the destruction of property, and
fearing worse might follow.

19.   The man was to prepare the way for a later visit of Jesus
to the district (vii. 31) and so was bidden to publish his cure.   In
Galilee, where He was teaching, notoriety would have hindered
Him.   See n. i. 44.

the Lord, in the O.T. sense, i.e. Jehovah, the God of Israel,
cf. Matt. xv. 31.

20.   **began,** for his preaching marked the beginning of an
important development.

Decapolis, the region about the E. and S. of the Lake.   It was
a loosely-used term for a group of Greek cities variously given.

did marvel.   Wonder now took the place of fear (15), and
they were better prepared for His second visit (vii. 31) when
some even confessed 'He has done all things well' (vii. 37).

    B.   (e).   Return to West side of the Lake.
    [*Matt. ix.* 18–31.   *Luke viii.* 40–56.]

21.   **the other side,** probably Capernaum once more.   See
Matt. ix. 18–25, where this incident occurs in a different context.
22.   **rulers of the synagogue,** officers who had the general

23 him, he falleth at his feet, and beseecheth him much,
saying, My little daughter is at the point of death : *I pray
thee*, that thou come and lay thy hands on her, that she
24 may be made whole, and live. And he went with him ;
and a great multitude followed him, and they thronged
him.

25 And a woman, which had an issue of blood twelve
26 years, and had suffered many things of many physicians,
and had spent all that she had, and was nothing bettered,
27 but rather grew worse, having heard the things concerning
Jesus, came in the crowd behind, and touched his gar-
28 ment. For she said, If I touch but his garments, I shall
29 be made whole. And straightway the fountain of her
blood was dried up ; and she felt in her body that she
30 was healed of her plague. And straightway Jesus, perceiving in himself that the power *proceeding* from him
had gone forth, turned him about in the crowd, and said,
31 Who touched my garments ? And his disciples said unto
him, Thou seest the multitude thronging thee, and sayest
32 thou, Who touched me ? And he looked round about to
33 see her that had done this thing. But the woman fearing

---

supervision of the services. A small synagogue had only one
ruler (Luke xiii. 14), a larger required several (Acts xiii. 15).

falleth. Note the humility of this man in high social position.

lay thy hands. This symbolic action was common among
the Jews, for blessing or healing (cf. Gen. xlviii. 14).

27. his garment, i.e. the 'hem' or blue cord which edged
the upper garment (see Num. xv. 38). Four tassels of white
wool hung at the corners of this garment, and perhaps one of
these was touched by the woman (cf. also Matt. xxiii. 5)[1].

28. she said, lit. 'kept saying,' showing the faith of the
sufferer.

31. his disciples. Luke attributes the hasty question to
Peter.

32. Jesus (whether He really knew the patient or not) wished
the woman to declare herself, that He might tell the immediate
reason of her cure (cf. i. 41, ii. 5, vi. 5, 6).

33. fearing, because her touch had made Him ceremonially
'unclean.' According to legend, Veronica was the name of the

[1] For the dress worn by our Lord, see Edersheim, *Life*, i. 620 foll.

and trembling, knowing what had been done to her, came
and fell down before him, and told him all the truth.
And he said unto her, Daughter, thy faith hath made 34
thee whole; go in peace, and be whole of thy plague.

While he yet spake, they come from the ruler of the 35
synagogue's *house*, saying, Thy daughter is dead: why
troublest thou the Master any further? But Jesus, not 36
heeding the word spoken, saith unto the ruler of the
synagogue, Fear not, only believe. And he suffered no 37
man to follow with him, save Peter, and James, and John
the brother of James. And they come to the house of 38
the ruler of the synagogue; and he beholdeth a tumult,
and *many* weeping and wailing greatly. And when he 39
was entered in, he saith unto them, Why make ye a
tumult, and weep? the child is not dead, but sleepeth.
And they laughed him to scorn. But he, having put them 40
all forth, taketh the father of the child and her mother
and them that were with him, and goeth in where the
child was. And taking the child by the hand, he saith 41
unto her, Talitha cumi; which is, being interpreted,

---

woman who was cured. A statue was erected in her honour at
Caesarea Philippi.

35. The raising of the widow's son at Nain (Luke vii. 11–17)
was not known in this neighbourhood.

36. Note the interesting variation here from the A. V.

37. Peter, and James, and John. These three of the 'inner
circle' were again His chosen companions at the Transfiguration
(ix. 2) and at Gethsemane (xiv. 33). *Here* He needed witnesses
from among His own disciples, whereas a crowd of noisy
spectators was out of place.

38. wailing. These were hired mourners, who cried aloud,
according to Oriental custom.

39. sleepeth. Jesus here uses figurative language, teaching
that death is not the end of life (cf. 1 Cor. xv. 18). This miracle
helped to prepare the disciples to accept the fact of the Resurrection; cf. n. on iv. 41.

they laughed, being professional mourners, who took Jesus'
words, denying the death, quite literally, and doubted His power.

41. Talitha cumi. The actual Aramaic words which were

42 Damsel, I say unto thee, Arise.   And straightway the
   damsel rose up, and walked ; for she was twelve years
   old.   And they were amazed straightway with a great
43 amazement.   And he charged them much that no man
   should know this : and he commanded that *something*
   should be given her to eat.

B. (*f*).   *Visit to Nazareth.*

6   And he went out from thence ; and he cometh into
2 his own country; and his disciples follow him.   And
   when the sabbath was come, he began to teach in the
   synagogue : and many hearing him were astonished,
   saying, Whence hath this man these things? and, What
   is the wisdom that is given unto this man, and *what*
3 *mean* such mighty works wrought by his hands?   Is not
   this the carpenter, the son of Mary, and brother of James,

---

used, for this was probably the dialect in which He habitually
spoke. Cf. vii. 34, xiv. 36.
   43. Jesus was leaving the district (vi. 1) and did not wish to
be hindered by the curious crowds whom the news would have
brought.

B. (*f*).   *Visit to Nazareth.*
[*Matt. xiii.* 54–58.   *? Luke iv.* 16–30.]

   VI. 1. his own country, i.e. Nazareth. See n. on i. 9.
The presence of His disciples showed that He came as a
Teacher, not privately.
   2. to teach. Luke (iv. 16–30) gives the address more fully ;
He read aloud and then explained a passage of the Jewish
Scriptures (see n. on i. 22). But Luke's account *may* refer to an
earlier occasion.
   the wisdom. Shown in His interpretation of Is. lxi. (Luke iv.
17–21).
   3. the carpenter. This makes it probable that Jesus followed
the trade of Joseph. (See Holman Hunt's picture 'The Shadow
of the Cross,' and Millais' 'Carpenter's Shop.') Mark never
mentions Joseph, who was probably dead before this time.
   James, etc. See n. on iii. 31. Nothing is known of Joses.
For Judas see n. on iii. 18. Simon only occurs here and in
Matt. xiii. 55. The 'sisters' are nowhere else mentioned.

and Joses, and Judas, and Simon? and are not his sisters
here with us? And they were offended in him. And 4
Jesus said unto them, A prophet is not without honour,
save in his own country, and among his own kin, and in
his own house. And he could there do no mighty work, 5
save that he laid his hands upon a few sick folk, and
healed them. And he marvelled because of their unbelief. 6

THIRD SECTION. [vi. 6*b*–vii. 23.]

C. (*a*). *Second Tour in Galilee: mission of the Twelve.*

And he went round about the villages teaching.

And he called unto him the twelve, and began to send 7
them forth by two and two; and he gave them authority
over the unclean spirits; and he charged them that they 8
should take nothing for *their* journey, save a staff only;
no bread, no wallet, no money in their purse; but *to go* 9

---

4. A prophet...in his own house. Possibly a proverb corresponding to our 'Familiarity breeds contempt.' Apparently
Jesus in His early days at Nazareth had not appeared remarkably different from other boys.

5. The faith of the patients, which was necessary to the cure,
was lacking, except in a few cases. See i. 41.

6. he marvelled, having in such matters only the ordinary
human means of knowledge. Cf. Matt. viii. 10.

C. (*a*). *Second Tour in Galilee: mission of the Twelve.*
[*Matt. ix.* 35–38, *x.* 1, 5–42, *xi.* 1. *Luke ix.* 1–6.]

teaching. Matt. (ix. 35) gives details of the tour; cf. i. 39.

7. began to send, for this was a 'new departure' in His
work. They were now to become apostles ('missionaries') as
well as disciples ('learners'), see n. on iii. 14. Matt. (x.) gives
details of their instructions.

two and two. Matt. in his list of the Twelve arranges them
in pairs (Matt. x. 2–4).

unclean spirits. Matt. and Luke add the commission to
preach and to heal disease.

8. a staff. Symbol of a traveller; cf. Jacob's words in
Gen. xxxii. 10.

purse, lit. 'girdle,' the folds of which were used as a pouch.

shod with sandals: and, *said he*, put not on two coats.
10 And he said unto them, Wheresoever ye enter into a
11 house, there abide till ye depart thence. And whatsoever
place shall not receive you, and they hear you not, as ye
go forth thence, shake off the dust that is under your feet
12 for a testimony unto them. And they went out, and
13 preached that *men* should repent. And they cast out
many devils, and anointed with oil many that were sick,
and healed them.

C. (b). The fame of Jesus reaches Herod.

14   And king Herod heard *thereof*; for his name had
become known: and he said, John the Baptist is risen

---

9. sandals. Another sign of the traveller; cf. Exod. xii. 11.

put not on. They might apparently (according to Mark)
take a change of clothes, but not enjoy the luxury of wearing
two 'under-garments' on the journey. (The English 'coats' is
misleading.)

10. thence, i.e. 'from that town or village.' Those who
refused hospitality (in the East an instinctive duty) would not be
likely to listen to the teaching.

11. shake off the dust. This symbolic act of rejection *may*
refer to the Jewish practice of wiping the feet on return from
foreign travels, as if to get rid of heathen defilement; in the
present case it would then symbolise the rejection of unbelievers
from the new Kingdom. See Acts xiii. 51.

a testimony, i.e. to teach them a lesson, not as a punishment;
cf. xiii. 9.

12. repent. Their work was to be like the *preliminary* work
of their Master on His first tour. Repentance was to be both
the text and result of their preaching.

13. cast out...devils. In this they failed sometimes (ix. 18)
through lack of faith.

anointed with oil. Oil was much used in medical treatment,
and so was made use of by the disciples as the symbol of healing,
and is still so used in the Roman Church. Perhaps also it was
meant to help the patient's faith by showing a willingness to cure
him (cf. vii. 33, viii. 23) [1].

C. (b). The fame of Jesus reaches Herod.
[Matt. xiv. 1–12. Luke ix. 7–9.]

14. king Herod, i.e. H. Antipas, 'tetrarch' (or ruler) of
Galilee and Peraea. See Introd. p. xxvii. The mission of the

[1] See also James v. 14.

from the dead, and therefore do these powers work in him.
But others said, It is Elijah. And others said, *It is* a 15
prophet, *even* as one of the prophets. But Herod, when he 16
heard *thereof*, said, John, whom I beheaded, he is risen.

[*C.* (*c*). *Parenthetical account of the Baptist's death.*]
For Herod himself had sent forth and laid hold upon 17
John, and bound him in prison for the sake of Herodias,
his brother Philip's wife: for he had married her. For 18
John said unto Herod, It is not lawful for thee to have
thy brother's wife. And Herodias set herself against 19

Twelve and the second tour in Galilee had spread the fame of
Jesus.

these powers, i.e. miraculous powers. Apparently John did
no miracles (cf. John x. 41), but men thought that now, if he
had come to life again, he might be endowed with miraculous
powers. Herod's remorse led him to believe that John was the
man they had heard of.

15. Elijah. Men expected him to reappear before the
Messiah came. See Mal. iv. 5, 6[1]; John i. 21. His mysterious
disappearance probably gave rise to the belief.

a prophet, i.e. 'one of the *great* prophets.' It was commonly
expected that Jeremiah would reappear[2]. Cf. Matt. xvi. 14.

[*C.* (*c*). *Parenthetical account of the Baptist's death.*]
[*Matt. xiv.* 1-12.]

17. Herod himself. He was responsible for John's imprisonment, but not *directly* for his death. The whole episode
refers to a time some way back. i. 14 alludes to the arrest,
which was before our Lord's ministry in Galilee began, though
John was preaching during the Judaean ministry. He was in
prison apparently during the period covered by i. 14–v. 13.

in prison, the fortress of Machaerus on the E. of the Dead Sea .

Herodias, wife of Philip (not the same as Philip the tetrarch),
half-brother to Herod Antipas, who divorced his own wife and
took Herodias away from Philip.

18. not lawful. Perhaps John sent disciples with the message
to Antipas when he was staying at the palace of Machaerus.

19. set herself against him, or, possibly, 'kept an eye on
him.'

[1] Stanley, *Jewish Church*, II. Lect. xxx.
[2] *Id. ibid.* 451.
[3] G. A. Smith, *H. G.* 569, 570.

20 him, and desired to kill him ; and she could not ; for
   Herod feared John, knowing that he was a righteous
   man and a holy, and kept him safe.   And when he heard
   him, he was much perplexed ; and he heard him gladly.
21 And when a convenient day was come, that Herod on his
   birthday made a supper to his lords, and the high cap-
22 tains, and the chief men of Galilee ; and when the daughter of Herodias herself came in and danced, she pleased
   Herod and them that sat at meat with him ; and the king
   said unto the damsel, Ask of me whatsoever thou wilt,
23 and I will give it thee.   And he sware unto her, Whatsoever thou shalt ask of me, I will give it thee, unto the half
24 of my kingdom.   And she went out, and said unto her
   mother, What shall I ask? And she said, The head of
25 John the Baptist.   And she came in straightway with
   haste unto the king, and asked, saying, I will that thou
   forthwith give me in a charger the head of John the Bap-
26 tist.   And the king was exceeding sorry ; but for the sake
   of his oaths, and of them that sat at meat, he would not
27 reject her.   And straightway the king sent forth a soldier

20. **he heard him,** probably sending for him at intervals, being
impressed by his power, though overborne later by his wife.
     Note variation from A. V. **much perplexed** for ‘ did many
things.’
     21. **a supper.**   Birthday feasts were perhaps imitated from a
custom of the Roman emperors.   The guests were here of three
classes, civil officials, military officers, and leading Galilean Jews.
     22. **the daughter of H.,** i.e. of Herodias and Philip.   Her
name was Salome, and she married later Philip the tetrarch.   It
was a special degradation for a *queen's* daughter to dance thus
before the men, and even the Greeks (from whom the Herods
borrowed the custom) did not allow any but slaves so to demean
themselves.
     23.   Cf. this verse with the story of Esther and Ahasuerus,
Esther v. 3.
     25. **with haste.**   The girl too had murderous wishes.
     forthwith.   The banquet must therefore have been at the
palace of Machaerus, close to the fortress.
     27. **a soldier of his guard,** a Lat. word (*speculator*), see
Introd. p. xiv.

of his guard, and commanded to bring his head: and he
went and beheaded him in the prison, and brought his 28
head in a charger, and gave it to the damsel; and the
damsel gave it to her mother. And when his disciples 29
heard *thereof*, they came and took up his corpse, and laid
it in a tomb.

C. (*d*).   *Return to the Lake: crossing to shore near Bethsaida.*

And the apostles gather themselves together unto 30
Jesus; and they told him all things, whatsoever they had
done, and whatsoever they had taught. And he saith 31
unto them, Come ye yourselves apart into a desert place,
and rest a while. For there were many coming and
going, and they had no leisure so much as to eat. And 32
they went away in the boat to a desert place apart. And 33
the people saw them going, and many knew *them*, and
they ran there together on foot from all the cities, and
outwent them. And he came forth and saw a great 34

---

28. his head. The cathedral of Amiens claims now to
possess it.

29. his disciples. The effects of John's preaching seem to
have lasted on for some time. See Acts xix. 3.

C. (*d*).   *Return to the Lake: crossing to shore near Bethsaida.*
[*Matt. xiv.* 13–21.   *Luke ix.* 10–17.   *John vi.* 1–14.]

30–44. The feeding of the 5000 is the *only* miracle recorded
by all four evangelists. Cf. John's account with its fuller details,
and the discourse founded on it.

30. the apostles, now 'envoys' and not merely 'learners,'
n. on iii. 14.

gather themselves, i.e. from various directions probably.

31. Come...apart, for rest and perhaps to avoid Herod. He
never saw Jesus till the day of His death. (Luke xxiii. 7–12.)

a desert place. Near Bethsaida Julias, N.E. of the Lake, a
town recently rebuilt by Herod Philip, and 4 m. across the water
from the supposed site of Capernaum.

33. outwent them, more probably 'anticipated them,' in the
sense of 'came before they were wanted,' thus breaking into His
retirement. The distance by land was 10 miles.

34. came forth, i.e. out of His retirement.

multitude, and he had compassion on them, because they were as sheep not having a shepherd : and he began to

35 teach them many things. And when the day was now far spent, his disciples came unto him, and said, The place is

36 desert, and the day is now far spent : send them away, that they may go into the country and villages round

37 about, and buy themselves somewhat to eat. But he answered and said unto them, Give ye them to eat. And they say unto him, Shall we go and buy two hundred

38 pennyworth of bread, and give them to eat? And he saith unto them, How many loaves have ye? go *and* see. And when they knew, they say, Five, and' two fishes.

39 And he commanded them that all should sit down by

40 companies upon the green grass. And they sat down in

41 ranks, by hundreds, and by fifties. And he took the five loaves and the two fishes, and looking up ⸱to heaven, he blessed, and brake the loaves ; and he gave to the

---

as sheep. A reminiscence of O.T. phrases. See Num. xxvii. 17 ; 1 Kings xxii. 17 ; Ezek. xxxiv. 6, etc.

36. country, rather, 'farms.'

37. pennyworth. A Lat. word (*denarius*) is used for the coin. See R.V. marg. on Matt. xviii. 28. The denarius was an ordinary day's wages (see Matt. xx. 2) and was nearer half-a-crown than a penny in value.

38. Five, and two fishes. These were supplied by a lad in the crowd (John vi. 9). The 'fish' were probably the dried salt fish which were the chief industry of the Lake, and were eaten as a relish.

39. green grass. This marks the time of year, for it is only in spring that the grass of the Jordan Valley is green. (Cf. John vi. 4.) The crowds were probably on their way to Jerusalem for the Passover.

40. in ranks, lit. 'a kitchen-garden bed,' or 'row of onions,' i.e. in regular groups or long rows, as vegetables are planted.

41. he took the five loaves, thus appearing to the people as their *host.*

he blessed, and brake. Cf. the language describing the Last Supper (xiv. 22). Perhaps this miracle prepared the disciples' minds for the teaching of that later Feast, the spiritual feeding of men with the 'bread of life.' John gives the discourse on the 'Living Bread' after this miracle. (John vi. 22-40.)

disciples to set before them ; and the two fishes divided
he among them all. And they did all eat, and were filled. 42
And they took up broken pieces, twelve basketfuls, and 43
also of the fishes. And they that ate the loaves were five 44
thousand men.

C. (e). *On the Lake: Jesus walks on the water.*

And straightway he constrained his disciples to enter 45
into the boat, and to go before *him* unto the other side to
Bethsaida, while he himself sendeth the multitude away.
And after he had taken leave of them, he departed into 46
the mountain to pray. And when even was come, the 47
boat was in the midst of the sea, and he alone on the

---

blessed, using probably the Jewish ' grace ':—" Blessed art
thou, O Lord our God, King of the world, who bringest forth
bread from the earth." By using this ' grace' Jesus would
testify to God as the Giver of all food, even of that supplied
through His own act. Cf. the incident of John xxi. 13[1].

43. broken pieces, i.e. not ' scraps,' but the surplus of what
He had broken up for distribution. The miracle of mercy taught
the disciples a lesson of carefulness. Jesus here made protest
(John vi. 12) against waste.

basketfuls. The basket here referred to was the strong wicker
kind carried by the poorer Jews in Rome on their backs. These
were probably the provision baskets of the Twelve. Possibly (37)
they often gave food to the poor.

C. (e). *On the Lake: Jesus walks on the water.*
[*Matt. xiv.* 22–26. *John vi.* 15–21.]

45. constrained his disciples. John (vi. 15) gives the explanation. It has been suggested that He feared lest His own
disciples should be infected by the people's wild desire to seize
and make Him king[2].

the other side, not of the Lake, but of a small bay, at one
end of which the 5000 had been fed. The disciples were to put
in at Bethsaida to take up Jesus for the voyage across the Lake.

46. them, i.e. the people, for the disciples had left.

to pray, as at other great crises of His career (cf. i. 35). Now
He had to face danger from Herod, and also the blind enthusiasm
of the people (n. on 45).

---

[1] Hort, *Village Sermons in Outline*, 252 foll. Edersheim, *Life*, I. 682, 683.
[2] Latham, *Pastor Pastorum*, 307.

48 land. And seeing them distressed in rowing, for the wind
was contrary unto them, about the fourth watch of the
night he cometh unto them, walking on the sea; and he
49 would have passed by them: but they, when they saw
him walking on the sea, supposed that it was an appari-
50 tion, and cried out: for they all saw him, and were
troubled. But he straightway spake with them, and
saith unto them, Be of good cheer: it is I; be not afraid.
51 And he went up unto them into the boat; and the wind
52 ceased: and they were sore amazed in themselves; for
they understood not concerning the loaves, but their
heart was hardened.

---

48. distressed, lit. 'tortured,' a very strong word. These
sudden gales are characteristic of lakes shut in by hills: n. on
iv. 37.

about the fourth watch, i.e. between 3 and 6 a.m., according to the Roman method of reckoning, which counted
four 'watches' between sunset and sunrise, beginning at 6 p.m.
(see xiii. 35). John (vi. 19) says they were halfway across the
Lake.

would have passed, i.e. 'feigned to,' as a test of their faith.

51. ceased, lit. 'grew weary,' as if the wind was personified
(cf. iv. 39); Matt. adds that Peter walked on the water to meet
Jesus.

amazed. Matt. records that they confessed He was 'Son of
God.' Cf. Peter's deliberate acknowledgment later on (viii. 29).
See also John i. 34, 49.

52. they understood not. The recent miracle had not opened
their eyes sufficiently to the boundless scope of His Power.

hardened (cf. iii. 5). They did not yet understand or wholly
believe in their Master. The miracle (as in the case of the
Transfiguration) was meant as an object-lesson to the disciples,
to teach them that Jesus was an '*ever-present*' help in trouble.
By such lessons He continually taught the disciples at this period,
preparing their minds for the after lessons of the Resurrection.
Cf. n. on iv. 41 [1].

---

[1] Latham, *Pastor Pastorum*, 91 foll., 305-310; *The Risen Master*,
62, 83.

C. (*f*).   *Landing at Plain of Gennesaret.*

And when they had crossed over, they came to the 53
land unto Gennesaret, and moored to the shore.   And 54
when they were come out of the boat, straightway *the
people* knew him, and ran round about that whole region, 55
and began to carry about on their beds those that were
sick, where they heard he was.   And wheresoever he 56
entered, into villages, or into cities, or into the country,
they laid the sick in the marketplaces, and besought him
that they might touch if it were but the border of his
garment: and as many as touched him were made whole.

And there are gathered together unto him the Phari- **7**
sees, and certain of the scribes, which had come from
Jerusalem, and had seen that some of his disciples ate 2
their bread with defiled, that is, unwashen, hands.   For 3

C. (*f*).   *Landing at Plain of Gennesaret.*
[*Matt. xiv.* 34-36 ; *xv.* 1-20.]

53. crossed over, i.e. to the W. shore: n. on 45.
Gennesaret. A small plain, then thickly populated, S. of
Capernaum, 3 m. long by 1 broad, and once very fertile[1]. Here
there would be no chance of 'retirement.'
56. border of his garment. The people may have heard of
the miracle recorded v. 27-29. During this visit should probably
be placed the Discourse on the Bread of Life (John vi. 22-59).
VII. 1-23. In the following incident there are three stages :
(1) The retort of Jesus to the Pharisees (1-13),
(2) His teaching to the *people*, in parabolic form, on the
ceremonial law (14, 15),
(3) His explanation of His words to the *disciples* indoors
(17-23).
1. Pharisees and...scribes. Cf. their hostility earlier (iii. 6,
22).
2. bread. Possibly the 'broken pieces' they had carried
away after the miracle.
defiled, that is, unwashen. A note for Mark's Gentile
readers. See Introd. p. xv. The *general* sense of the word
translated 'defiled' is merely 'unconsecrated.'
3-5. The rules for ceremonial washing were absurdly elaborate,

---

[1] G. A. Smith, *H. G.* 443 n. Stanley, *Sinai and Palestine*, 374.

the Pharisees, and all the Jews, except they wash their hands diligently, eat not, holding the tradition of the
4 elders : and *when they come* from the marketplace, except they wash themselves, they eat not : and many other things there be, which they have received to hold, wash-
5 ings of cups, and pots, and brasen vessels. And the Pharisees and the scribes ask him, Why walk not thy disciples according to the tradition of the elders, but eat
6 their bread with defiled hands ? And he said unto them, Well did Isaiah prophesy of you hypocrites, as it is written,

> This people honoureth me with their lips,
> But their heart is far from me.
7 But in vain do they worship me,
> Teaching *as their* doctrines the precepts of men.
8 Ye leave the commandment of God, and hold fast the

---

e.g. sometimes a second washing was necessary to remove any possible defilement from the water of the first !

3. all the Jews, i.e. not one sect only. Another note for Gentile readers.

diligently, or, 'up to the elbow,' or, 'with the fist,' i.e. the water was poured over the clenched fist, to 'cleanse' the whole hand[1].

the elders, i.e. the great Rabbis of a former age, whose interpretations of the Law were as sacred as the Law itself.

4. the marketplace, where they might rub up against a Gentile in the crowds.

wash themselves (see R.V. marg.). Perhaps = ' bathe themselves.'

5. walk. This verb (for 'live') has become a common metaphor.

6. The answer is in two parts (6–8, 9–14), each beginning with the same phrase.

you hypocrites. This was the Pharisees' usual charge against the Sadducees.

it is written. A free adaptation from Is. xxix. 13.

8. 'You neglect God's Law, and follow man's interpretation of it.' The spirit of the Law (as given in Deut.) is love to God and one's neighbour.

[1] Edersheim, *Life*, II. 10, 11.

tradition of men. And he said unto them, Full well do ye 9
reject the commandment of God, that ye may keep your
tradition. For Moses said, Honour thy father and thy 10
mother ; and, He that speaketh evil of father or mother,
let him die the death : but ye say, If a man shall say to 11
his father or his mother, That wherewith thou mightest
have been profited by me is Corban, that is to say, Given
to God ; ye no longer suffer him to do aught for his father 12
or his mother ; making void the word of God by your 13
tradition, which ye have delivered : and many such like
things ye do. And he called to him the multitude again, 14
and said unto them, Hear me all of you, and understand :
there is nothing from without the man, that going into 15
him can defile him : but the things which proceed out of
the man are those that defile the man. And when he was 17
entered into the house from the multitude, his disciples
asked of him the parable. And he saith unto them, Are 18

---

9. 'You not only *neglect* God's Law, but *run counter* to it.'
The example follows in 10.

10. Moses said. The 5th commandment. Ex. xx. 12 and
xxi. 17.

11. Corban = 'a consecrated gift'; an Aramaic word (cf.
v. 41). If such a gift was used for ordinary purposes it brought
a curse (see Josh. vii.). In order to keep his goods out of his
parents' hands a man would apparently pretend they were
'consecrated' and therefore could not be touched by them
with impunity.

12. ye no longer suffer him, i.e. 'you thus make it *illegal* for
him to support his parents.'

13. making void, i.e. 'making it a dead-letter.'

14, 15. 'Outward' and 'inward' here correspond to 'material'
and 'spiritual.'

15. Jesus here attacks the Law itself, by abolishing the
distinction between 'clean' and 'unclean' food, and laying
down in its stead the principle of spiritual purity. St Paul seems
to have known of this discourse, his teaching in Col. ii. 16—iii. 11
closely follows it. Jesus' method was to state *principles*, for His
followers to ponder over and apply. The A.V. here inserts
an extra verse, 'If any man hath ears to hear, let him hear.'

17. the parable, or rather, 'mysterious saying.' See iii. 23.

ye so without understanding also? Perceive ye not, that
whatsoever from without goeth into the man, *it* cannot
19 defile him ; because it goeth not into his heart, but into
his belly, and goeth out into the draught? *This he said,*
20 *making all meats clean.* And he said, That which pro-
21 ceedeth out of the man, that defileth the man. For from
within, out of the heart of men, evil thoughts proceed,
22 fornications, thefts, murders, adulteries, covetings, wickednesses, deceit, lasciviousness, an evil eye, railing, pride,
23 foolishness : all these evil things proceed from within,
and defile the man.

The explanation to the disciples is private. (Cf. iv. 11.) Matt.
gives the effect upon them of the Master's bold words (Matt. xv.
12–14).

18, 19. An explanation of the Scribes' confusion of spiritual
with bodily purity. The body can only be affected by material
things, such as food and water.

19. This he said. The Revisers' addition, to make it clear
that the last four words of the verse are a note by the writer, who
had himself grasped the principle. Peter took long to learn it.
(Acts x.) The adoption in the R. V. of a better reading brings
out the point (wholly missed by the A. V.) that it is Jesus who
' makes all meats clean.'

21. evil thoughts, which include all sins, for Jesus taught
that men are judged by motives rather than acts. The first
plural in the list is *general,* the others indicate separate acts
of sin.

22. covetings. The high moral code of Jesus, as also that
of Moses (10th commandment), counts this weakness a crime.
Cf. 1 Cor. vi. 10.

wickednesses, i.e. malicious acts or intentions.

deceit, a vice characteristic of the Jews.

lasciviousness. Profligacy was characteristic of the Gentiles,
and especially of the Greeks.

an evil eye, metaphorical for 'jealousy,' 'the bearing of a
grudge.'

pride, the special vice of the Pharisees.

foolishness, as opposed to 'wisdom' in the broad O.T. sense
(see Prov. i. 7, iv. 5–9, etc.). Vice and folly are often identified
in the Bible.

IN NORTHERN GALILEE.

FIRST SECTION. [vii. 24—viii. 26.]

D. (a). Retirement to Phoenicia: cure of a Gentile.

And from thence he arose, and went away into the 24
borders of Tyre and Sidon. And he entered into a house,
and would have no man know it: and he could not be
hid. But straightway a woman, whose little daughter 25
had an unclean spirit, having heard of him, came and fell
down at his feet. Now the woman was a Greek, a Syro- 26
phœnician by race. And she besought him that he would
cast forth the devil out of her daughter. And he said 27
unto her, Let the children first be filled: for it is not meet
to take the children's bread and cast it to the dogs. But 28
she answered and saith unto him, Yea, Lord: even the
dogs under the table eat of the children's crumbs. And 29
he said unto her, For this saying go thy way; the devil is

D. (a). Retirement to Phoenicia: cure of a Gentile.

[*Matt. xv.* 21–25.]

24. he arose. The phrase implies removal to a quite
different district. This was a retirement from danger, and
henceforward He was less seen in public.

borders of Tyre, i.e. Phoenicia, at this period a long strip of
sea-coast and plain, with heathen anti-Jewish inhabitants, though
some had already sought Jesus (iii. 8). The cure He performed
here was to indicate the eventual inclusion of the Gentiles in His
Kingdom.

26. a Greek, i.e. a Greek-speaking woman of the old
Phoenician race, 'Canaanites' of the O.T. Since the Roman
conquest by Pompey, Phoenicia had been reckoned as part of
Syria.

27. the children, i.e. the Jews. Perhaps Jesus is quoting
a Jewish proverb, showing their scornful attitude towards the
Gentiles.

28. Matt. gives more details of the conversation.

29. For this saying. Because it showed her faith, which was
necessary to the cure. (Cf. i. 40, iii. 5, v. 34, etc.) Our Lord
acted thus (*a*) to test the woman, (*b*) to show that His mission was
primarily to the Jews. Contrast the faith of this Gentile and
the hostility of the Scribes in the Plain of Gennesaret.

30 gone out of thy daughter.   And she went away unto her
house, and found the child laid upon the bed, and the
devil gone out.

D. (b).   Return to East side of the Lake : cure of a deaf mute.

31   And again he went out from the borders of Tyre, and
came through Sidon unto the sea of Galilee, through the
32 midst of the borders of Decapolis.   And they bring unto
him one that was deaf, and had an impediment in his
speech; and they beseech him to lay his hand upon him.
33 And he took him aside from the multitude privately, and
put his fingers into his ears, and he spat, and touched his
34 tongue ; and looking up to heaven, he sighed, and saith
35 unto him, Ephphatha, that is, Be opened.   And his ears
were opened, and the bond of his tongue was loosed, and

D. (b).   Return to East side of the Lake: cure of a deaf mute.

31. again he went out, probably following the great road
which led from Phoenicia across the Leontes and over the
Lebanon to Damascus, but leaving it at Caesarea Philippi to
turn south.   This long journey would give the apostles rest
(see vi. 31), and delay the return till the people were somewhat
quieted down.

Sidon.   Originally the capital of Phoenicia, but eclipsed by
Tyre from Solomon's time onwards.

unto the sea of Galilee, i.e. to the E. side of the Lake.
Decapolis includes the whole district E. of the Lake, sometimes
even as far N. as Damascus.   Jesus had hitherto only paid it a
flying visit, and alarmed the people (v. 17).

33, 34.   A gradual cure, as in the case of the blind man
(viii. 23-26), both miracles related by Mark only.   Possibly the
man's *deafness* was the reason of this gradual method; he could
only be taught by signs, and it was essential he should *understand* the cure, that his own faith might be called forth.   Cf. v. 30,
ix. 29, for other instances that Jesus did not *easily* work His
cures.

33. he spat.   Saliva was popularly used in cures, perhaps as
a sort of charm.   Jesus used it as symbolical of healing.   Cf.
viii. 23; John ix. 6.

34. he sighed, weighed down by the burden of suffering
humanity.

Ephphatha.   An Aramaic word: n. on v. 41.

he spake plain. And he charged them that they should 36
tell no man: but the more he charged them, so much the
more a great deal they published it. And they were 37
beyond measure astonished, saying, He hath done all
things well: he maketh even the deaf to hear, and the
dumb to speak.

D. (c). Four thousand fed: return to the West shore.

In those days, when there was again a great multi- **8**
tude, and they had nothing to eat, he called unto him his
disciples, and saith unto them, I have compassion on the 2
multitude, because they continue with me now three days,
and have nothing to eat: and if I send them away fasting 3
to their home, they will faint in the way; and some of
them are come from far. And his disciples answered 4
him, Whence shall one be able to fill these men with
bread here in a desert place? And he asked them, How 5
many loaves have ye? And they said, Seven. And he 6

---

37. Matt. (xv. 29) adds that many other cures were done in
this region.

D. (c). Four thousand·fed: return to West shore.

[*Matt. xv.* 32–38.]

VIII. 1–10. It is not probable that this story is only another
version of the feeding of the 5000, for the details differ throughout (see foll. notes)[1]. No doubt the same lesson was taught by
both miracles, before to the Jews of Capernaum, and now to the
(perhaps mainly Gentile) crowd at Decapolis (see Matt. xv. 31).

1. again a great multitude (cf. with A.V.). This crowd
had not (like the 5000) followed from a distance, but had
collected as Jesus passed through the villages of the district,
having now laid aside their first fears (v. 17), perhaps on account
of the cured demoniac's teaching (v. 20).

2. continue with me now three days. Cf. vi. 35, 'the
day....'

4. Whence...etc. Before there had been lack of money;
now the difficulty is to procure food at all. The disciples' forget-
fulness and lack of faith are often referred to in the Gospels.

[1] Edersheim (*Life*, II. 63) suggests why both miracles are recorded: see
also Plumptre on Matt. xv. 32–39; Westcott, *Characteristics of the Gospel
Miracles*, Serm. i.

commandeth the multitude to sit down on the ground:
and he took the seven loaves, and having given thanks,
he brake, and gave to his disciples, to set before them;
7 and they set them before the multitude. And they had a
few small fishes: and having blessed them, he commanded
8 to set these also before them. And they did eat, and
were filled: and they took up, of broken pieces that
9 remained over, seven baskets. And they were about four
10 thousand: and he sent them away. And straightway he
entered into the boat with his disciples, and came into
the parts of Dalmanutha.

D. (d). *The Pharisees demand a sign.*

11 And the Pharisees came forth, and began to question
with him, seeking of him a sign from heaven, tempting
12 him. And he sighed deeply in his spirit, and saith, Why
doth this generation seek a sign? verily I say unto you,
13 There shall no sign be given unto this generation. And

---

8. seven baskets. Before there had been twelve, apparently
the private possession of the disciples. Here a different Greek
word for 'basket' is used (cf. vi. 43); these were large hampers
or crates. (The word occurs Acts ix. 25.)

10. the boat, evidently put ready for Him by some means,
as they had come by *land*.

Dalmanutha. Matt. (xv. 29) mentions Magadan. Both were
probably small villages, but nothing is known of them.

D. (d). *The Pharisees demand a sign.*
[Matt. xv. 39—xvi. 4.]

11. came forth, apparently from Dalmanutha.

a sign. They desired some sensational display of supernatural
power, such as the O.T. heroes had given[1], but Jesus had early
put aside this temptation (Matt. iv. 5). Healing they thought
could be done by magic or the help of evil spirits.

tempting him, i.e. putting Him to the test, if He really *were*
the Messiah or no.

12. verily I say. See n. on iii. 28.

---

[1] Edersheim (*Life*, I. 68, 69) gives curious illustrations.

he left them, and again entering into *the boat* departed to the other side.

> *D.* (*e*). *Discourse* (*in the boat*) *on the leaven of the Pharisees and of Herod.*

And they forgot to take bread ; and they had not in 14 the boat with them more than one loaf. And he charged 15 them, saying, Take heed, beware of the leaven of the Pharisees and the leaven of Herod. And they reasoned 16 one with another, saying, We have no bread. And Jesus 17 perceiving it saith unto them, Why reason ye, because ye have no bread? do ye not yet perceive, neither understand? have ye your heart hardened? Having eyes, see 18 ye not? and having ears, hear ye not? and do ye not remember? When I brake the five loaves among the five 19 thousand, how many baskets full of broken pieces took

---

13. the other side, from the mention (22) of Bethsaida, this must mean the N. shore.

> *D.* (*e*). *Discourse* (*in the boat*) *on the leaven of the Pharisees and of Herod.*
>
> [*Matt. xvi.* 5–12.]

14. they forgot. Judas Iscariot was probably the caterer (John xii. 6).

15. leaven. Except in Matt. xiii. 33 this metaphor is always used in the Bible for some *evil* influence, as showing the great effects produced secretly by something very small in itself. The 'leaven of the Pharisees' is the spirit of their teaching, which working subtly amongst men produces merely *external* religion (cf. Luke xii. 1). The 'leaven of the Sadducees' is their worldliness, which produces irreligion. Matt. mentions the presence of Sadducees with the deputation, and gives the warning as uttered against their leaven also.

16. they reasoned, heedlessly taking His words as literal, regardless of the meaning.

18. Having eyes, etc. An allusion to Jer. v. 21, where *spiritual* blindness and deafness are described. Cf. also iv. 12.

19, 20. how many...took ye up? They would remember their own part in each incident. For 'baskets' see R.V. marg. and n. on viii. 8.

CH. 4

20 ye up? They say unto him, Twelve. And when the
seven among the four thousand, how many basketfuls of
broken pieces took ye up? And they say unto him, Seven.
21 And he said unto them, Do ye not yet understand?

D. (f). At Bethsaida: cure of a blind man.

22   And they come unto Bethsaida. And they bring to
23 him a blind man, and beseech him to touch him. And he
took hold of the blind man by the hand, and brought him
out of the village; and when he had spit on his eyes, and
laid his hands upon him, he asked him, Seest thou aught?
24 And he looked up, and said, I see men; for I behold *them*
25 as trees, walking. Then again he laid his hands upon his
eyes; and he looked stedfastly, and was restored, and
26 saw all things clearly. And he sent him away to his
home, saying, Do not even enter into the village.

---

21. Do ye not yet understand? He has given them hints,
and leaves them to work out the answer, according to His usual
method of teaching[1]. Thought would show them (1) that the
'leaven' was a metaphor, (2) that they must ponder over the
lesson involved in its use, (3) that it was faithless to doubt His
power after such a miracle. Matt. gives more details of the
lesson.

D. (f). At Bethsaida: cure of a blind man.

22. Bethsaida, n. on vi. 45.
23. This and the miracle in vii. 31-37 are the only ones
peculiar to St Mark. See n. on vii. 34 for the use of saliva.
Probably Jesus wrought the cure gradually, and used a familiar
remedy, to help the man's faith. Where the patient's faith was
perfect, He healed with a word, and at once.
the village, probably in the district of Bethsaida.
24. as trees, i.e. with vague, blurred outlines.
26. sent him...to his home. To think quietly over his
experience before spreading the news abroad. Cf. ii. 11,
v. 19. A.V. adds, 'neither tell it to any in the town.'

[1] Latham, *Pastor Pastorum*, esp. 5, 6.

SECOND SECTION. [viii. 27–ix. 50.]

E. (a). Expedition to region of Caesarea Philippi.

And Jesus went forth, and his disciples, into the 27
villages of Cæsarea Philippi : and in the way he asked
his disciples, saying unto them, Who do men say that
I am? And they told him, saying, John the Baptist : and 28
others, Elijah ; but others, One of the prophets. And he 29
asked them, But who say ye that I am? Peter answereth
and saith unto him, Thou art the Christ. And he charged 30
them that they should tell no man of him. And he began 31
to teach them, that the Son of man must suffer many
things, and be rejected by the elders, and the chief priests,

---

E. (a). Expedition to region of Caesarea Philippi.
[*Matt. xvi.* 13–28. *Luke ix.* 18–27.]

27. The ministry in Galilee was nearly over, and Jesus may
have desired comparative solitude in which to further teach its
lessons to the disciples.

Cæsarea, near the source of the Jordan, rebuilt by Herod
Philip, and called after him (second name) and the Emperor
Augustus [1].

28. Cf. nn. on vi. 14, 15.

29. the Christ, lit. 'the Anointed'; in the O.T. applied to
a king or a priest; the word is the Greek equivalent for 'Messiah.'
Matt. (xvi. 17) adds the reply of Jesus, that Peter is the rock
on which the Church shall be founded. Mark omits this answer,
perhaps by Peter's wish. See Introd. p. xvi.

30. tell no man of him. The news that the Messiah had
actually come would have created a popular rising, and thus
have prevented or hastened His Passion.

31. began to teach, i.e. this was a new topic to the disciples.
See i. 45 and Matt. xvi. 21. **Son of man**, n. on ii. 10.

suffer many things. The second Isaiah (Is. liii.) had foretold
a suffering Messiah, but the Jews had not understood the teaching,
and thought only of a successful King.

The three classes of the Sánhedrin are here enumerated :

elders, ordinary well-to-do citizens, such men perhaps as
Nicodemus and Joseph of Arimathea, cf. xv. 43.

chief priests, including the high priest, who presided over
the Council, the ex-high priests, and other leading priests.

[1] Stanley, *Sinai and Palestine*, 397. Edersheim, *Life*, II. 72–74.

and the scribes, and be killed, and after three days rise
32 again. And he spake the saying openly. And Peter
33 took him, and began to rebuke him. But he turning
about, and seeing his disciples, rebuked Peter, and saith,
Get thee behind me, Satan: for thou mindest not the
34 things of God, but the things of men. And he called
unto him the multitude with his disciples, and said unto
them, If any man would come after me, let him deny him-
35 self, and take up his cross, and follow me. For whosoever would save his life shall lose it; and whosoever shall

---

scribes, n. on i. 22.

32. openly, i.e. no longer in parables or dark sayings. See John xvi. 25, 29.

took him, i.e. in a patronizing way, perhaps unduly elated by the great promise just made to him (n. on 29).

33. seeing his disciples, teaching them by the rebuke of Peter and probably including them in it, Peter being their spokesman.

Satan. Peter's suggestion was the old temptation (Matt. iv. 9) in a new form. It reappeared in the Garden of Gethsemane, and was a third time conquered (xiv. 36).

The rebuke to Peter is a dramatic contrast to the words of promise just spoken (n. on 29). Its sternness shows that Jesus here regarded Peter as the tool of Satan, made use of to provoke Him to sin.

34. he called...the multitude, for *all* His followers must hear the lesson of suffering that His service entails.

deny himself, i.e. sink his own personality altogether.

take up his cross. The Romans made a condemned criminal carry his own cross to the place of execution (see John xix. 17). The words mean therefore 'let him be ready to face the utmost shame, to die like a despised criminal,' as his Master will do. Peter himself is said to have literally fulfilled these words. See John xxi. 19, 20.

35-37. A difficult lesson to understand fully. The choice which lay before the first disciples was between desertion of Jesus and a violent death. He therefore warns them, (1) That safety through desertion was worse than death, for it meant the destruction of 'life,' in its highest sense. (2) He shows the relation of the bodily 'life' to the highest 'life,' death being but the gateway to complete and more real 'life.'

35. whosoever would save his life, etc. A saying of our

lose his life for my sake and the gospel's shall save it. For what doth it profit a man, to gain the whole world, 36 and forfeit his life? For what should a man give in 37 exchange for his life? For whosoever shall be ashamed 38 of me and of my words in this adulterous and sinful generation, the Son of man also shall be ashamed of him, when he cometh in the glory of his Father with the holy angels. And he said unto them, Verily I say unto you, **9** There be some here of them that stand *by*, which shall in no wise taste of death, till they see the kingdom of God come with power.

Lord's on several other occasions (Matt. x. 39; Luke xvii. 33. Cf. John xii. 25).

life. The word is used for 'the principle of life,' but men (Jesus implies) call by the name of 'life' that which is not truly life in any complete sense of the word. (See note above on the whole passage.)

for my sake and the gospel's. Devotion to Christ is devotion to the service of man.

36. what doth it profit... ? An appeal to the disciples' own hearts: they *know* that within the man is something more precious than anything outside him. Perhaps Jesus has still in His thoughts Satan's offer of sovereignty. (Matt. iv. 9, see n. on 33.)

38. Paraphrase :—'Anyone refusing discipleship on these terms of mine (34), will at the last be rejected by Me when I come as Messiah in glory.'

the glory of his Father, etc..., i.e. with *spiritual* glory rather than earthly material splendour, as the Jews expected the Messiah to come.

IX. 1. unto them. Probably it is to the disciples alone that He gives this reassuring promise, perhaps in reply to some query of theirs.

the kingdom of God come with power. The prophecy was fulfilled in several ways, e.g. in the rapid spread of the 'news of the Kingdom' after Christ's Ascension, and again in the Fall of Jerusalem 40 years later. The words contain the germ of the prophecy in xiii., and the lesson taught is that the disciples rightly expected signs of power in the Messiah, but were wrong in looking for material splendour at His appearing.

E. (b). The Transfiguration.

2 And after six days Jesus taketh with him Peter, and
James, and John, and bringeth them up into a high
mountain apart by themselves : and he was transfigured
3 before them : and his garments became glistering, exceeding white ; so as no fuller on earth can whiten them.
4 And there appeared unto them Elijah with Moses : and
5 they were talking with Jesus. And Peter answereth and
saith to Jesus, Rabbi, it is good for us to be here : and let

---

E. (b). The Transfiguration.
[Matt. xvii. 1-13. Luke ix. 28-36.]

2. The writer evidently intends to contrast the prophecy of
the Passion with this scene of glory and heavenly vision.

These three chosen disciples were with Jesus also at the
raising of Jairus's daughter (v. 37) and in Gethsemane (xiv. 33).

a high mountain, unidentified, but possibly a spur of Mount
Hermon, whose snow-capped summit is visible from many
heights of Palestine. The presence of a 'crowd' (14) is however somewhat against such a distant site, and suggests that the
company had returned to Galilee. The traditional site, Mount
Tabor, is very improbable, since at this time there was a fortress
on the top of it, nor is there any indication that Jesus was in that
region.

transfigured. Cf. the description of Moses, Ex. xxxiv. 29.

3. exceeding white. A.V. adds ' as snow.'

4. Elijah with Moses, representing perhaps the Prophets
and the Law.

Both died mysteriously (Deut. xxxiv. 6 ; 2 Kings ii. 11), and
Elijah was expected to reappear (cf. viii. 28), while there are
traces of a similar belief about Moses.

were talking. Luke (ix. 31) says the vision came while
Jesus was praying, and that the topic of conversation was His
coming Passion. The appearance taught the disciples the
harmony between His sufferings and His glory, and showed
them the relation of the earlier revelation to His own teaching,
preparing them once more for His death and final victory ; see
n. on iv. 41.

5. Apparently Peter wished to prolong the vision, perhaps
that others might share it with them. See the ref. to this event
2 Pet. i. 16 foll., and possibly in John i. 14.

us make three tabernacles; one for thee, and one for
Moses, and one for Elijah. For he wist not what to 6
answer; for they became sore afraid. And there came a 7
cloud overshadowing them : and there came a voice out
of the cloud, This is my beloved Son : hear ye him. And 8
suddenly looking round about, they saw no one any more,
save Jesus only with themselves.

E.   (*c*).   *Descent from the mountain : question about Elijah's*
coming.

And as they were coming down from the mountain, he 9
charged them that they should tell no man what things
they had seen, save when the Son of man should have
risen again from the dead. And they kept the saying, 10
questioning among themselves what the rising again from
the dead should mean. And they asked him, saying, The 11

---

tabernacles, booths of branches, such as were made for the
Feast of Tabernacles.

7. a cloud. This symbol of God's presence occurs in the
O.T. during the Exodus (Ex. xvi. 10, xix. 9, xxiv. 15, etc.) and
at the dedication of the first Temple (1 Kings viii. 10). Cf. in
the N.T. the account of the Ascension (Acts i. 9) and the prediction of the Second Coming (Mark xiii. 26). Cf. Ps. civ. 3,
Is. xix. 1.

a voice, cf. the account of the Baptism (i. 11) when the
disciples were not present. To the witness then given is added
now the command "Hear ye him." The words were needed to
strengthen the disciples' faith in the days of trial that were
coming.

E.   (*c*).   *Descent from the mountain : question about Elijah's*
coming.

[*Matt. xvii.* 9–13.]

9. Secrecy was enjoined for a time, for such a vision would
have been in the early days misunderstood by the majority of His
followers.

10. Compare this questioning with their apparent inatten-
tion when once before (viii. 31) He spoke of His Resurrection.
Now they were forced to think of His meaning, when the
mysterious event of the future was to be the limit of their
silence.

12 scribes say that Elijah must first come. And he said
   unto them, Elijah indeed cometh first, and restoreth all
   things : and how is it written of the Son of man, that he
13 should suffer many things and be set at nought? But
   I say unto you, that Elijah is come, and they have also
   done unto him whatsoever they listed, even as it is written
   of him.

E.   (d).   At the foot of the mountain : cure of a demoniac boy.

14   And when they came to the disciples, they saw a great
   multitude about them, and scribes questioning with them.
15 And straightway all the multitude, when they saw him,
   were greatly amazed, and running to him saluted him.
16 And he asked them, What question ye with them? And
17 one of the multitude answered him, Master, I brought

---

11. The scribes say, literally interpreting Mal. iv. 5. Jesus
explains that the *spirit* of the prophecy was fulfilled in the
coming of John the Baptist, and further points out that the Jews
ignored the prophecies which foretold His sufferings, though
these too would be fulfilled.

12. restoreth all things. The Baptist brought back men
to the right attitude for receiving the Messiah. Cf. Luke i. 17.

13. This *v.* implies that the Jews will treat the Messiah as
they did the new 'Elijah'—cf. the parallel account in Matt.
xvii. 12.

as it is written. Perhaps an allusion to the intended murder
of Elijah by Jezebel (1 Kings xix. 2), foreshadowing the deed of
Herodias. The words may however refer generally to the
constant lesson of Scripture, the perfecting of God's servants
through suffering.

E.   (d).   At the foot of the mountain: cure of a demoniac boy.

[Matt. xvii. 14–21.   *Luke ix.* 37–43.]

14. Note the contrast between the glorious vision and this
scene of suffering below. Raphael, with a true instinct, represented both scenes in one picture.

15. amazed. Perhaps there was something unusual in His
manner, or else they were simply startled by His unexpected
approach. It is most improbable that His face still wore traces
of the transfiguring radiance, for the vision was not yet to be
known.

unto thee my son, which hath a dumb spirit ; and where- 18
soever it taketh him, it dasheth him down : and he foam-
eth, and grindeth his teeth, and pineth away : and I spake
to thy disciples that they should cast it out ; and they
were not able.   And he answereth them and saith, O 19
faithless generation, how long shall I be with you? how
long shall I bear with you? bring him unto me.   And 20
they brought him unto him : and when he saw him,
straightway the spirit tare him grievously ; and he fell on
the ground, and wallowed foaming.   And he asked his 21
father, How long time is it since this hath come unto him?
And he said, From a child.   And oft-times it hath cast 22
him both into the fire and into the waters, to destroy
him : but if thou canst do anything, have compassion on
us, and help us.   And Jesus said unto him, If thou canst ! 23
All things are possible to him that believeth.   Straight- 24
way the father of the child cried out, and said, I believe ;
help thou mine unbelief.   And when Jesus saw that 25
a multitude came running together, he rebuked the
unclean spirit, saying unto him, Thou dumb and deaf
spirit, I command thee, come out of him, and enter no
more into him.   And having cried out, and torn him 26
much, he came out : and *the child* became as one dead ;

---

18.   The symptoms suggest those of epilepsy.
19.   O faithless generation.   The reproach apparently includes the bystanders, the father, and the disciples.
21.   These questions show that Jesus depended for such
knowledge on ordinary sources of information.
22.   it hath cast him, i.e. the boy had tried in his fits to
commit suicide.
23.   The R.V. gives our Lord's reproachful quotation of the
man's doubting words (cf. with the A.V.).   Once more Jesus
shows that faith is necessary if the cure is to be performed,
cf. i. 41, vi. 5, 6, etc.
25.   a multitude came running.   Either these were fresh
people arriving, or Jesus had taken the man aside at first.
26.   A final violent attack, showing that the cure was not
magically effected by the mere presence of Jesus, but only when
the conditions of cure were satisfied.

27 insomuch that the more part said, He is dead. But Jesus took him by the hand, and raised him up; and he arose. 28 And when he was come into the house, his disciples asked 29 him privately, *saying*, We could not cast it out. And he said unto them, This kind can come out by nothing, save by prayer.

E. (e). *Return through Galilee: the Passion again foretold.*

30 And they went forth from thence, and passed through Galilee; and he would not that any man should know it. 31 For he taught his disciples, and said unto them, The Son of man is delivered up into the hands of men, and they shall kill him; and when he is killed, after three days he 32 shall rise again. But they understood not the saying, and were afraid to ask him.

E. (f). *At Capernaum again: discourses to the disciples.*

33 And they came to Capernaum: and when he was in the house he asked them, What were ye reasoning in the

---

29. This kind probably means the whole class of maladies called 'possession.' The disciples had again regarded the healing power as magic art, needing no special preparation on their part or answering faith; cf. i. 41, ii. 5, vi. 5. The A.V. (following many authorities) inserts "and fasting" after "prayer."

E. (e). *Return through Galilee: the Passion again foretold.*

30. from hence, i.e. presumably from the region of Caesarea Philippi. Probably He wished to use this journey as an opportunity of quiet instruction to the disciples [1].
31. The Son of Man, n. on ii. 10.
32. were afraid. They shrank from further information on an unwelcome subject, as before (viii. 33).

E. (f). *At Capernaum again: discourses to the disciples.*
[*Matt. xviii.* 1–9. *Luke ix.* 46–50.]

33. the house. Probably Peter's, or Levi's: cf. i. 29, ii. 15.

[1] Latham, *Pastor Pastorum,* 351.

way? But they held their peace: for they had disputed 34
one with another in the way, who *was* the greatest. And 35
he sat down, and called the twelve; and he saith unto
them, If any man would be first, he shall be last of all,
and minister of all. And he took a little child, and set 36
him in the midst of them: and taking him in his arms, he
said unto them, Whosoever shall receive one of such little 37
children in my name, receiveth me: and whosoever
receiveth me, receiveth not me, but him that sent me.

John said unto him, Master, we saw one casting out 38
devils in thy name: and we forbade him, because he
followed not us. But Jesus said, Forbid him not: for 39
there is no man which shall do a mighty work in my
name, and be able quickly to speak evil of me. For he 40

---

34. they had disputed. Possibly on account of the recent
distinction given to the 'chosen three' (ix. 2) or to Peter
(viii. 29). The Jews looked for a material kingdom, with many
distinctions of rank [1].

35. he sat down, i.e. assuming the attitude of a teacher.

minister. The Greek word denotes one who does the hum-
blest offices. Cf. the further teaching in x. 44. The recognition
of the duty of service owed by masters, rulers, etc. to those
under them is a sign of the growth of the Kingdom.

36. a...child. Perhaps one of Peter's children. Late tradition says it was St Ignatius.

37. one of such little children, i.e. 'anyone of a simple
and childlike character.' To recognize such is to know Christ.

receiveth not me... The language recalls phrases in St John's
Gospel.

38-40. A digression, after which (in 41) the discourse is
resumed.

38. John's conscience was apparently moved by the last
words of Jesus, and he felt bound to confess that they had not
'received' a would-be follower.

39. Forbid him not. Jesus counsels *tolerance*, and goes on
to show the possibilities of ·good in such a man. Cf. Moses'
answer to Joshua's protest against the 'prophesying' of Eldad
and Medad, Num. xi. 29.

40. There is apparent conflict here with the saying in
Matt. xii. 30 (Luke xi. 23), "He that is not with me is against

[1] Edersheim, *Life*, II. 116.

41 that is not against us is for us. For whosoever shall give
   you a cup of water to drink, because ye are Christ's, verily
42 I say unto you, he shall in no wise lose his reward. And
   whosoever shall cause one of these little ones that believe
   on me to stumble, it were better for him if a great millstone were hanged about his neck, and he were cast into
43 the sea. And if thy hand cause thee to stumble, cut it
   off : it is good for thee to enter into life maimed, rather
   than having thy two hands to go into hell, into the

---

me, and he that gathereth not with me scattereth " : but the contexts of the two sayings show that there is no real contradiction.

There the question is between those who do and those who
do not the work of Christ. *Here* it is between two classes, both
of whom do His work, viz. disciples and non-disciples ; the latter
class do His work, without recognizing that it is His.

41. For refers back to the argument of 37, ' Blessed is he
who receives a disciple in the name of Jesus, and however slight
may be the service done, his reward is great.'

Christ's. He now uses the title, because they recognize Him
as the Messiah (viii. 29). Hitherto they had known Him only as
Jesus.

verily I say unto you. Note on iii. 28.

42. The reverse of helping a brother is here shown, the
awful sin of tempting him to do evil. The ' little one ' is evidently
still present, and is used as a type of the ' weaker brethren.'
Cf. S. Paul's application of this teaching in 1 Cor. viii. and
Rom. xiv.

42. a great millstone—see R.V. marg.

43-47. Part of this passage occurs also in the Sermon on the
Mount (Matt. v. 29, 30) ; the lesson taught is an expansion of
the saying about the ' mote ' and the ' beam.' The duty of a
disciple towards *himself* is now the subject of the discourse.
The ' hand,' the ' foot,' and the ' eye ' stand for things good and
useful in themselves, but which when misused are best dispensed
with. The possible applications of the three ' stumbling-blocks '
are numerous. For instance artistic gifts (the ' hand ' or ' eye ')
may lead a man from the higher life, if he misuses them, or allows
them to divert his aim.

43. life, lit. ' the life,' i.e. the best kind of life.

hell. Greek Gehenna. The name of the ravine S.W. of
Jerusalem (the Hebrew Valley of Hinnom or Ge Hinnom)
where the worst of the Jewish kings carried on the worship
of Moloch. Josiah ' desecrated ' it (2 Kings xxiii. 10) and it

unquenchable fire. And if thy foot cause thee to stumble, 45
cut it off : it is good for thee to enter into life halt, rather
than having thy two feet to be cast into hell. And if thine 47
eye cause thee to stumble, cast it out : it is good for thee
to enter into the kingdom of God with one eye, rather
than having two eyes to be cast into hell ; where their 48
worm dieth not, and the fire is not quenched. For every 49
one shall be salted with fire. Salt is good : but if the salt 50
have lost its saltness, wherewith will ye season it ? Have
salt in yourselves, and be at peace one with another.

---

became the place where all the refuse of the city was thrown
out and burnt. The Rabbis used 'Gehenna' as a symbol of the
fate of the wicked, and our Lord adopted it as a metaphor for
the worst punishment (Matt. v. 22). The sense here is 'He who
will not sacrifice a part to save the whole, may end in destroying
his own soul.'

47. the kingdom of God, i.e. the 'realm' where the will of
God is done.

48. This *v.* is repeated in some MSS. as a refrain after 43 and
45. Cf. A.V. and R.V. for the whole passage 43—48. The
quotation is from Is. lxvi. 24, a prophecy of the fate of certain
apostates. The 'worm',is a metaphor for inward corruption, the
'fire' for external destruction ; both stand for *natural* means of
dissolution, not penalties imposed by someone else. The sense
is, 'Such a man condemns himself to eternal depravation and
destruction of his soul.'

49. This *v.* takes up the idea of 'fire' and applies it anew
to the purification of man's soul through the cleansing fire of the
Holy Spirit—(see Matt. iii. 11).

salted. Salt was used largely in Jewish sacrifices for
purification. (See Lev. ii. 13.) The A.V. gives here an explanatory 'gloss' (q.v.).

50. Salt is good. A fresh thought, suggested by the
reference to salt in the last *v.* The phrase occurs Luke xiv. 34,
in another context. (Cf. also Matt. v. 13.) They were to be
the 'salt of the earth,' to purify mankind, but how could this be
if their own purity of aim was sullied by self-seeking ? (see 34).
(The record of this difficult discourse is perhaps fragmentary, and
the thread of connexion may have been imperfectly preserved.)

Have salt in yourselves. A return to the subject which
had suggested the discourse, the dispute for pre-eminence. The
disciples must be pure if they are to purify others, and must
be at peace one with another. (Salt is the Eastern symbol of

X. 1–51.

PART II.   SKETCH OF JOURNEYS IN PERAEA AND JUDAEA.

(*a*).   *Final departure from Galilee: question of divorce.*

10   And he arose from thence, and cometh into the
borders of Judæa and beyond Jordan : and multitudes
come together unto him again ; and, as he was wont, he
2 taught them again.   And there came unto him Pharisees,
and asked him, Is it lawful for a man to put away *his*
3 wife? tempting him.   And he answered and said unto
4 them, What did Moses command you ?   And they said,
Moses suffered to write a bill of divorcement, and to put
5 her away.   But Jesus said unto them, For your hardness

---

hospitality, and perhaps this is the link here between 'salt' and
'peace.')

This discourse closes the Galilean ministry.

(*a*).   *Final departure from Galilee : question of divorce.*

[*Matt. xix.* 1–12.]

X. 1. he arose from thence.   The phrase indicates a departure to a different district (cf. vii. 24).

the borders of Judæa.   A vague heading to this period of
several months, of which Mark only records three incidents.
John records two visits to Jerusalem (John vii. 14, x. 22) apparently during this period; Luke gives various other events,
included in the section ix. 51—xviii. 34.

as he was wont, i.e. in parables, many of which are recorded
by Luke.

tempting him, rather 'testing,' by a clever question, hoping
to betray Him into disloyalty to Moses.   Cf. their previous
attacks, vii. 5, viii. 11.   They may have heard of His teaching
on divorce in the great Sermon (Matt. v. 32).   It was a question
which divided the two 'schools' of the Pharisees, and possibly
they wished also to involve Him in trouble with Herod Antipas,
who had divorced his wife in order to marry Herodias.

3.   He read their thoughts, and at once made reference to
Moses.

4.   suffered, i.e. Moses *allowed* divorces, but it was only a
concession.

The ref. is to Deut. xxiv. 1.

5.   For your hardness of heart.   Moses made the concession for their ancestors, whose moral standard was lower than

of heart he wrote you this commandment. But from the 6
beginning of the creation, Male and female made he
them. For this cause shall a man leave his father and 7
mother, and shall cleave to his wife ; and the twain shall 8
become one flesh : so that they are no more twain, but
one flesh. What therefore God hath joined together, let 9
not man put asunder. And in the house the disciples 10
asked him again of this matter. And he saith unto them, 11
Whosoever shall put away his wife, and marry another,
committeth adultery against her : and if she herself shall 12
put away her husband, and marry another, she committeth adultery.

(b). *Children blessed.*

And they brought unto him little children, that he 13
should touch them : and the disciples rebuked them.
But when Jesus saw it, he was moved with indignation, 14
and said unto them, Suffer the little children to come unto

---

their own, belonging as it did to an earlier age. His rule was
not meant therefore to be an ideal or permanent law, for the
moral teaching of the O.T. is clearly shown to be 'progressive'
throughout.

6–8. From Gen. i. 27, ii. 24. Jesus refers back to the
original idea of marriage, as set forth at the Creation, to show
that it was meant to be a permanent tie.

11. Jesus in private emphasises to His disciples the teaching
just given, declaring the marriage of divorced persons to be a
deadly sin, though it was sanctioned by Greek and Roman law.
According to Matt. (v. 32, xix. 9) He made one exception to
the rule.

(b). *Children blessed.*
[*Matt. xix.* 13–15. *Luke xviii.* 15–17.]

13. It was the custom thus to bring children to the rulers of
synagogues to be blessed. Jesus did more, for He embraced
them as well.

rebuked them, apparently thinking it below their Master's
dignity.

14. Nowhere else do we find Jesus moved to anger except
in the incident recorded in iii. 5.

me ; forbid them not : for of such is the kingdom of God.
15 Verily I say unto you, Whosoever shall not receive the
kingdom of God as a little child, he shall in no wise enter
16 therein. And he took them in his arms, and blessed them,
laying his hands upon them.

(c). The rich and the kingdom of God.

17 And as he was going forth into the way, there ran one
to him, and kneeled to him, and asked him, Good Master,
18 what shall I do that I may inherit eternal life? And Jesus
said unto him, Why callest thou me good? none is good
19 save one, *even* God. Thou knowest the commandments,
Do not kill, Do not commit adultery, Do not steal, Do
not bear false witness, Do not defraud, Honour thy father
20 and mother. And he said unto him, Master, all these
21 things have I observed from my youth. And Jesus looking upon him loved him, and said unto him, One thing

---

15, 16. Again He teaches the need of childlike simplicity
and humility in His followers (cf. ix. 36, foll.), and at the same
time shows His own deep tenderness.

(c). The rich and the kingdom of God.
[*Matt. xix.* 16–29. *Luke xviii.* 18–30.]

17. one, a young ruler, as we learn from Matthew and
Luke.

eternal life. The Rabbis taught belief in a future life, and
the doctrine had developed remarkably among the Jews after
the Captivity.

18. good. The man had used it merely as a term of respect.
Jesus takes the epithet and compels him to consider its real force;
his own idea of 'goodness' had been mere obedience to the
letter of the Law. Matt.'s version of the conversation (xix. 16,
17) is different, but the point is the same.

19. the commandments. He quotes those belonging to the
'Duty to our neighbour.' The reference to defrauding is perhaps specially introduced for one who had 'great possessions.' It
probably stands for the 10th Commandment here. (See Ex. xxi.
10; Deut. xxiv. 14.)

20. observed, i.e. literally kept them, like St Paul in his
early days (Phil. iii. 6).

thou lackest : go, sell whatsoever thou hast, and give to
the poor, and thou shalt have treasure in heaven : and
come, follow me. But his countenance fell at the saying, 22
and he went away sorrowful : for he was one that had
great possessions. And Jesus looked round about, and 23
saith unto his disciples, How hardly shall they that have
riches enter into the kingdom of God! And the disciples 24
were amazed at his words. But Jesus answereth again,
and saith unto them, Children, how hard is it for them
that trust in riches to enter into the kingdom of God! It 25
is easier for a camel to go through a needle's eye, than for
a rich man to enter into the kingdom of God. And they 26
were astonished exceedingly, saying unto him, Then who

---

21. sell...give to the poor. The spirit of love to our
neighbour underlies the letter of the Law, as Jesus taught also in
the Sermon on the Mount (Matt. vi. 21–37) and in answer to
the Scribe's question in xii. 30, 31. Here we see brought out
the difference between the bare Duty of the O.T. and the higher
ideal of Service found in the N.T. The actual command here
applies of course *literally* only to this particular case, but the
principle remains for all Christians (cf. ix. 43–48).

treasure in heaven. Cf. the parable of the Hidden Treasure,
Matt. xiii. 44; Luke xii. 33.

22. sorrowful. It is clear that he longed to obey, but
found the sacrifice too great. Perhaps later he may have found
courage, and followed the example of other well-to-do men in
the early days of the Church at Jerusalem. See Acts iv. 32–35.

23. Jesus, as often, reads the disciples a lesson from the
incident.

24. amazed. In spite of all His teaching, their ideas about
the Kingdom were still crude and vague, and riches would seem
to them a passport to entrance thither rather than a hindrance.

Children. The affectionate word shows His sympathy with
their perplexity.

for them that trust in riches. These six words should probably be omitted : they do not occur in the best texts and they
weaken the sense. The saying thus repeated is a general statement of the difficulty for *anyone*, though it is especially great
for the rich.

25. A proverbial saying for something impossible. Cf. the
Eng. proverb 'to make ropes of sand.'

CH.   5

27 can be saved? Jesus looking upon them saith, With men
it is impossible, but not with God : for all things are
28 possible with God. Peter began to say unto him, Lo, we
29 have left all, and have followed thee. Jesus said, Verily I
say unto you, There is no man that hath left house, or brethren, or sisters, or mother, or father, or children, or lands,
30 for my sake, and for the gospel's sake, but he shall receive
a hundredfold now in this time, houses, and brethren, and
sisters, and mothers, and children, and lands, with perse-
31 cutions; and in the world to come eternal life. But many
that are first shall be last; and the last first.

---

27. He arrests their attention by His gaze, before proceeding
to explanation. God could so move the rich man that the sacrifice
which to the young ruler had seemed 'impossible' would become possible through His grace. Cf. Luke xix, where the
story of the rich Zacchaeus who readily followed Jesus follows
this incident almost immediately. Note also Christ's deep
sympathy with the responsibilities of the rich.

28. **Peter began.** A new turn in the conversation, as Peter
reminds the Lord, with characteristic frankness, that he and the
other disciples *have* made the sacrifice required.

29-31. The Lord blesses their devotion, but adds a solemn
warning.

29. **Verily I say unto you.** n. on iii. 28.

30. **now in this time,** i.e. by the new converts who will be
added to the 'family' of the Church, they will gain 'brothers
and sisters,' while the Church itself will acquire new 'houses' and
'lands.' Cf. Acts iv. 34.

eternal life, sought by the young ruler (18) and claimed by
Peter as a reward for sacrifice.

31. **many that are first shall be last.** The saying is illustrated in Matt. xix. 30, xx. 16 by the parable of the Labourers in
the Vineyard and is repeated by Luke (xiii. 30) in another context.
It is a quiet rebuke to the self-seeking spirit of Peter, and its
truth was proved by his fall (xiv. 71), and by the treachery of
Judas. The second half of the saying was proved true by the
life of Paul, at first a persecutor, then an apostle.

(d). Journey towards Jerusalem : Passion foretold a third time.

And they were in the way, going up to Jerusalem ; and 32 Jesus was going before them : and they were amazed ; and they that followed were afraid.　And he took again the twelve, and began to tell them the things that were to happen unto him, *saying*, Behold, we go up to Jerusalem ; 33 and the Son of man shall be delivered unto the chief priests and the scribes ; and they shall condemn him to death, and shall deliver him unto the Gentiles : and they 34 shall mock him, and shall spit upon him, and shall scourge him, and shall kill him ; and after three days he shall rise again.

(d). Journey towards Jerusalem : Passion foretold a third time.

[*Matt. xx.* 17–19.　*Luke xviii.* 31–34.]

32.　in the way, i.e. one of the high-roads of the pilgrims from Peraea to Jerusalem, crossing the Jordan to the S. of Jericho, and thence by a steep ascent leading up into the Judaean hills[1].

amazed, evidently from something in the Master's manner, such as His walking before them (cf. Luke ix. 51).　His policy was now changed ; instead of avoiding notice He was eager to reach Jerusalem and meet His enemies, who had been lately roused by the miracle wrought on Lazarus (John xi. 47–57).

they that followed, i.e. probably the pilgrims from Galilee and Peraea.

took again, in contrast to His former 'going on before.'

33.　He reports with more definite words the prediction already made near Caesarea Philippi (viii. 31) and in Galilee. *Now* He wishes to show them that He knows the issue of the journey, and thus to reassure them.

Son of man. n. on ii. 10.

chief priests and the scribes. nn. on viii. 31 ; i. 22.

These represented the Temple and the Law respectively, and the phrase is an informal expression for the Sanhedrin, or national council, which tried religious questions and certain civil questions.　It could pass a sentence of death, but could not carry it out.

the Gentiles, lit. 'the nations' (i.e. 'the Romans') as opposed to 'the people,' i.e. Israel.　Cf. Ps. ii. 1 ; Acts iv. 27.

[1] G. A. Smith, *H. G.* 263 foll.

(e).   *The disciples' quarrel for precedence.*

35 And there come near unto him James and John,
the sons of Zebedee, saying unto him, Master, we would
that thou shouldest do for us whatsoever we shall ask of
36 thee.   And he said unto them, What would ye that I
37 should do for you?   And they said unto him, Grant unto
us that we may sit, one on thy right hand, and one on *thy*
38 left hand, in thy glory.   But Jesus said unto them, Ye
know not what ye ask.   Are ye able to drink the cup that
I drink? or to be baptized with the baptism that I am
39 baptized with?   And they said unto him, We are able.
And Jesus said unto them, The cup that I drink ye shall
drink; and with the baptism that I am baptized withal

(e).   *The disciples' quarrel for precedence.*

[*Matt. xx.* 20–28.]

35. James and John.   Matt. records that Salome, their
mother, made the request.   Possibly her relationship to Jesus
prompted the petition, or else the prominence which had been
already given to her sons and Peter on several occasions.   Luke
xviii. 34 shows that they did not yet at all understand the
prediction of the Passion.

37.   The petition was for the places of honour at a king's
court.

in thy glory.   They still wholly misunderstood the nature
of His Kingdom, and thought this journey to the capital was
undertaken in order to declare Himself King.

38.   the cup...the baptism, metaphors suggested by the
petition itself: the 'cup' belongs to a royal banquet, and the
'baptism' possibly alludes to the luxurious baths which the
Herods had introduced, after the Roman custom.   For Christ's
'courtiers' these royal luxuries become respectively a bitter
draught and a plunge into the bracing waters of affliction; cf. for
similar uses of these metaphors xiv. 36; Ps. lxxv. 9; Luke xii. 50;
Ps. xviii. 16.   The sense then is—'Can you face the sufferings
which are the privileges of my court?'

39. We are able.   Cf. with this too self-reliant loyalty St
Paul's words, "I can do all things *in him that strengtheneth me*."
(Phil. iv. 13.)

ye shall drink.   James was put to death by Herod Agrippa I
(Acts xii. 2); John was exiled to Patmos, and both had previously
lived through the perilous early days of the Church.

shall ye be baptized : but to sit on my right hand or on *my* 40
left hand is not mine to give : but *it is for them* for whom
it hath been prepared. And when the ten heard it, they 41
began to be moved with indignation concerning James
and John. And Jesus called them to him, and saith unto 42
them, Ye know that they which are accounted to rule over
the Gentiles lord it over them; and their great ones exer-
cise authority over them. But it is not so among you : 43
but whosoever would become great among you, shall be
your minister : and whosoever would be first among you, 44
shall be servant of all. For verily the Son of man came 45
not to be ministered unto, but to minister, and to give his
life a ransom for many.

---

40. not mine to give. Christ is no eastern despot to
distribute favours at will. His servants must *win* their places in
His Kingdom.

41. moved with indignation, not because their own ideas
as to the Kingdom were any higher or truer, but because they
resented the presumption of their companions.

42, 43. Four grades are mentioned, rulers, nobles, servants,
slaves.

42. those...accounted to rule. The phrase suggests that the
appearance of authority and the reality are not always found
together. In Christ's kingdom, i.e. among men looked upon
with eyes opened by Him, "the meek inherit the earth."
Thus Queen Victoria ruled the hearts of her people because
she 'served' them.

43. He that desires the second rank (see n. on 42, 43) must
seek the third, he that wishes for the first must become as the
slave, or lowest.

45. the Son of man. n. on ii. 10.

a ransom. The subjects must submit to the *life* of a slave,
but the King submits to the *death* of a slave, thus far surpassing
them in self-surrender. Later He illustrates this further by
washing the disciples' feet (John xiii. 1–11). The impression
made on at least one of the two ambitious disciples is seen from
John's account of the Last Supper (John xiii.), and from the
whole tenor of his writings.

(*f*).   *Near Jericho: blind Bartimaeus healed.*

46   And they come to Jericho: and as he went out from
Jericho, with his disciples and a great multitude, the son
of Timæus, Bartimæus, a blind beggar, was sitting by the
47 way side.   And when he heard that it was Jesus of Nazareth, he began to cry out, and say, Jesus, thou son of
48 David, have mercy on me.   And many rebuked him,
that he should hold his peace : but he cried out the more
a great deal, Thou son of David, have mercy on me.
49 And Jesus stood still, and said, Call ye him.   And they
call the blind man, saying unto him, Be of good cheer:
50 rise, he calleth thee.   And he, casting away his garment,
51 sprang up, and came to Jesus.   And Jesus answered him,
and said, What wilt thou that I should do unto thee? And
the blind man said unto him, Rabboni, that I may receive

(*f*).   *Near Jericho: blind Bartimaeus healed.*
[*Matt. xx.* 29-34.   *Luke xviii.* 35-43.]

46.   they come, possibly by a road from the city of Ephraim.
See John xi. 54.
went out from.   Probably by the main road[1] from Jericho to
Jerusalem.   Luke (xix. 2-10) adds the story of Zacchaeus and
the parable of the Pounds.
Jericho.   About 5 miles from the Jordan, and 15 from Jerusalem.   Jesus here came deliberately within the power of Pontius
Pilate (see Introd., p. xxvii.) and of the Sanhedrin.
a great multitude, i.e. of Jews going up to the Passover.
Jesus no longer shunned publicity, for there was no longer need
to hide Himself, now that He was going to Jerusalem to die.
Bartimæus, i.e. 'son of Timaeus.'   The full description
suggests that in consequence of his cure he may have become a
well-known person.   Matt.'s account gives *two* blind men, Luke
places the incident on the way *into* the town.
47.   son of David, a title of the Messiah, showing the
beggar's recognition of the Christ.   His faith brought about his
cure (*v.* 52); cf. vi. 5, 6.
51.   Rabboni.   An Aramaic word, a more respectful form
of the familiar 'Rabbi' and only used in addressing a learned
scribe.   Mary of Magdala used it at the tomb (John **xx.** 16).

[1] G. A. Smith, *H. G.* 264.

my sight. And Jesus said unto him, Go thy way; thy 52
faith hath made thee whole. And straightway he received
his sight, and followed him in the way.

XI. 1—XV. 47.

PART III. THE LAST WEEK.

(a). *1st day: entry into Jerusalem, and return to Bethany.*

And when they draw nigh unto Jerusalem, unto Beth- 11
phage and Bethany, at the mount of Olives, he sendeth
two of his disciples, and saith unto them, Go your way 2
into the village that is over against you : and straightway

The beggar's use of it again showed his recognition of One
greater than the mere teacher and healer whom the simple folk
reverenced.

52. straightway. Cf. this instantaneous cure with the
gradual cure of the blind man at Bethsaida (viii. 22–26). See
n. on viii. 23.

(a). *1st day: entry into Jerusalem, and return to Bethany.*

[*Matt. xxi.* 1–11. *Luke xix.* 29–44. *John xii.* 12–19.]

XI. 1. See n. on xiv. 3–9.
Bethphage. The site of this village is unknown.
Bethany, a village on the side of the Mt of Olives farthest
from Jerusalem, and the home of Jesus' friends, Martha, Mary,
and Lazarus[1]. (John xi.) Its modern name is El Azarieh or
Lazari, probably from Lazarus's name. Here Jesus slept these
four nights, for at the Passover season the villages round Jerusalem were filled with pilgrims.
mount of Olives. The E. slope of this hill is 3 m. from
Jerusalem. Hence David took his last view of the city (2 Sam.
xv. 30).
2. the village, possibly Bethphage. If so, it must have
been between Bethany and Jerusalem, on the W. slope of the
hill.
The ass was to be one never yet ridden upon, a condition
which marks the sacred character and kingly state of the Rider,
who now claims the honour and recognition which He has
hitherto avoided. See n. on 10.

[1] Stanley, *Sinai and Palestine*, 185–195.

as ye enter into it, ye shall find a colt tied, whereon no
3 man ever yet sat ; loose him, and bring him. And if any
one say unto you, Why do ye this ? say ye, The Lord hath
need of him ; and straightway he will send him back
4 hither. And they went away, and found a colt tied at the
5 door without in the open street ; and they loose him. And
certain of them that stood there said unto them, What do
6 ye, loosing the colt ? And they said unto them even as
7 Jesus had said : and they let them go. And they bring
the colt unto Jesus, and cast on him their garments ; and
8 he sat upon him. And many spread their garments upon
the way ; and others branches, which they had cut from
9 the fields. And they that went before, and they that
followed, cried, Hosanna ; Blessed *is* he that cometh in

---

3.   The message implies that the owner knew and acknowledged 'The Master.'

7.   garments.   Cf. the proclamation of Jehu 2 Kings ix.
13.

8.   branches, lit. 'mats,' i.e. of leaves, grass, etc., a green
carpet spread before the Conqueror. John mentions 'palm-
branches' carried by the people, whence the familiar name
'Palm-Sunday.'

9.   The remembrance of Jesus riding on the ass suggested in
after days to the disciples the Messianic prophecy of Zech. ix. 9.
See John xii. 16. The ass was the ordinary riding animal of the
great and wealthy. Cf. Judges v. 10.

they that went before.   Probably a second crowd which
had come out from the city to meet the procession. Those that
'followed' were the pilgrims who had come from Jericho and
beyond (x. 46).

Hosanna, lit. 'Save now.'   A Hebrew greeting to the
Saviour. The quotation is from Ps. cxviii. 26, the last of the
group (cxiii.–cxviii.) which formed the Hallel, a festival hymn
used especially at the Passover (see xiv. 26)[1]. Also the last five
verses were used to greet the pilgrims as they arrived.

he that cometh, a phrase often used for the Messiah who
'was to come.' Cf. Matt. xi. 3. The people therefore welcomed
Jesus as a Passover pilgrim, but also recognized in Him the
Messiah.

---

[1] Edersheim, *Life*, II. 367, 368.

the name of the Lord : Blessed *is* the kingdom that com- 10
eth, *the kingdom* of our father David : Hosanna in the
highest. And he entered into Jerusalem, into the temple ; 11
and when he had looked round about upon all things, it
being now eventide, he went out unto Bethany with the
twelve.

---

10. Apparently some of the crowd add these words to the
usual greeting ; Mark alone records them. They show that the
people expected a literal restoration of David's kingdom, con-
necting with this idea Jesus' frequent phrases 'the kingdom of
God,' 'the kingdom of Heaven [1].'

The crowd now accepts Jesus as the Messiah, and expects
Him to manifest His power at the Passover by some great
miracle (as Satan had long ago suggested to Him). The
enthusiasm rapidly died away when no such 'sign' was given,
though a hint is given in xiv. 2 of the attitude of many of the
people, but they lacked a leader. Jesus allowed this public
'triumph' that it might in after days teach the people the lesson
of His real triumph as King of Peace, in spite of apparent defeat.
The Transfiguration, the Last Supper, and many of the miracles
were in the same way 'acted parables,' to teach men the meaning of Christ's life on earth, as seen in the light thrown back
upon it by the Death and Resurrection. The contrasts of
triumph and humiliation in this week illustrate Christ's own
saying in ix. 35.

11. he entered into Jerusalem. Probably the shouts burst
forth at the first sight of the city : then from a certain point on
the ridge of Olivet the city and glittering new Temple came into
view, and here probably Jesus uttered His lament (Luke xix.
41–44)[2]. Thence the procession descended, crossed the Kidron
valley, and dispersed below the Temple hill, for the pilgrims to
cleanse themselves from travel stains. No doubt they told the
great news in the city (Matt. xxi. 10), causing anxiety to the
rulers, who would fear a popular rising, such as was not infrequent at the Passover season, when vast numbers of Jews were
assembled.

into the temple, i.e. into the court of the Gentiles, which He
would face on coming up from the Kidron valley[3]. He no longer
seeks to avoid publicity, for the crisis has come. See xi. 2.

looked round about, i.e. taking note of the abuses which on
the morrow He was to condemn.

---

[1] See further on this passage, Swete's notes in loc. and reff.
[2] Stanley, *Sinai and Palestine*, 192, 193.
[3] Edersheim, *The Temple*, ch. i., ii.

(b). 2nd day : walk into Jerusalem.

12   And on the morrow, when they were come out from
13 Bethany, he hungered.   And seeing a fig tree afar off
having leaves, he came, if haply he might find anything
thereon : and when he came to it, he found nothing
14 but leaves ; for it was not the season of figs.   And he
answered and said unto it, No man eat fruit from thee
henceforward for ever.   And his disciples heard it.

15   And they come to Jerusalem : and he entered into the
temple, and began to cast out them that sold and them
that bought in the temple, and overthrew the tables of the
money-changers, and the seats of them that sold the
16 doves ; and he would not suffer that any man should
17 carry a vessel through the temple.   And he taught, and

(b). 2nd day: walk into Jerusalem.

[*Matt. xxi.* 18-19 a, 12-17.   *Luke xix.* 45-48.]

13. having leaves. The earliest figs ripen in June, and this
was but April ; but the fruit is often eaten unripe with bread,
and as the fruit is formed *before* the leaves, there was reason for
expecting to find at least unripe figs under the leaves.

14. from thee. The half-personification is characteristically
oriental, cf. iv. 39.

15. began to cast out, assuming priestly authority. The
priests were responsible for these abuses, and were therefore
indignant.   John (ii. 13-27) records another cleansing, at the
beginning of the Ministry.

them that sold, i.e. those who sold victims for sacrifice in the
outer court.

the money-changers, i.e. those who supplied the Jewish
money required for the Temple offerings.   The 'changers' are
said to have made excessive profits out of the transaction.

the doves, i.e. those required on such occasions as that described in Luke ii. 24.

16. carry a vessel, i.e. make a short cut through the Temple
courts, which was illegal, but commonly done.   Jesus showed
that He had come to purify, not destroy, the national religion,
yet He was accused (xiv. 58) of blasphemy against the Temple.
Apparently there was little resistance made, owing probably to
His tone and look of ' authority.'

17. Quotation from Is. lvi. 7.

said unto them, Is it not written, My house shall be called a house of prayer for all the nations? but ye have made it a den of robbers. And the chief priests and the scribes 18 heard it, and sought how they might destroy him: for they feared him, for all the multitude was astonished at his teaching.

And every evening he went forth out of the city. 19

(c). 3rd day: (i) *walk into Jerusalem.*

And as they passed by in the morning, they saw the 20 fig tree withered away from the roots. And Peter calling 21 to remembrance saith unto him, Rabbi, behold, the fig tree which thou cursedst is withered away. And Jesus 22 answering saith unto them, Have faith in God. Verily 23

---

for all the nations. The 'court of the Gentiles' was intended for their devotions, but the traffic made it useless for that purpose. The second Isaiah prophesied the growth of the Jewish religion into a universal religion: hence his prediction that the Temple should be resorted to by all nations. See Is. lvi. and lx.

a den of robbers, fulfilling the words of Jeremiah (Jer. vii. 11). The chief priests were as 'robbers,' seizing the Son's inheritance: bandits rather than 'thieves,' as in the A. V. Cf. John x. 8.

18. chief priests and the scribes. Note on x. 33. The priests resented His interference in the Temple, the Scribes were jealous of the freshness and popularity of His teaching.

19. every evening, i.e. from Sunday to Wednesday inclusive.

(c). 3rd day: (i) *walk into Jerusalem.*
[*Matt. xxi.* 19 *b*–22.]

20. passed by, i.e. on their way into Jerusalem from Bethany.

21. Rabbi, behold.... Peter wishes for some explanation, or perhaps he merely exclaims in surprise at the destruction of the tree which had been cursed; the words used by Jesus had not necessarily implied the tree's immediate death.

22. Have faith in God. The miracle was an answer to a prayer of faith, and in itself it was also a lesson, an acted parable. The strangeness of the miracle startled the disciples, as it was meant to do; they would now remember its lesson, as in that other startling case of the destruction of the swine (v. 13). The fig-tree with its show of leaves and lack of fruit was like the Jewish nation with its gorgeous Temple, exact observance of the Law, and its conspicuous want of spiritual faith. The lesson

I say unto you, Whosoever shall say unto this mountain,
Be thou taken up and cast into the sea ; and shall not
doubt in his heart, but shall believe that what he saith
24 cometh to pass ; he shall have it.   Therefore I say unto
you, All things whatsoever ye pray and ask for, believe
that ye have received them, and ye shall have them.
25 And whensoever ye stand praying, forgive, if ye have
aught against any one ; that your Father also which is in
heaven may forgive you your trespasses.

(*d*).   3*rd day* (*continued*)*:* (ii) *in the Temple-courts.*

27   And they come again to Jerusalem : and as he was
walking in the temple, there come to him the chief priests,

---

then for the disciples is, ' See that you have the faith which your
rulers have not, for with that you may overcome obstacles which
seem impossible to overcome[1].'   The miracle forms part of the
double conflict of the last days, in which while the Jews are
rejecting and condemning Jesus, He meanwhile is rejecting
and condemning them.   This is seen in (*a*) the sign of the
withered fig-tree, (*b*) The parable of the Vineyard (xii. 1-12),
(*c*) The prophecy of national calamity (xiii. 5-37).   Luke records
a fig-tree parable (Luke xiii. 6-9).

23. Verily I say unto you, n. on iii. 28.

to this mountain.   Cf. Luke xvii. 6.   Jesus adopts a figurative saying common among the Rabbis, who described a great
teacher as 'a rooter-up of mountains.'   The apostles removed
'mountains' of difficulty by their faith in the early days of the
Church.   See also Zech. xiv. 4.

24, 25.   Christ warns them however (1) that this faith must be
expressed in faithful prayer, (2) that they must pray with
humility and love, not *against* but *for* their fellow-men.   Cf.
S. Paul's words 1 Cor. xiii. 2.

25. stand, the usual Jewish attitude of prayer, cf. Luke xviii.
11, 13.

your Father...etc.   The language would recall to them His
former lesson on prayer.   (Matt. vi. 12, 14 foll.)

(*d*).   3*rd day* (*continued*)*:* (ii) *in the Temple-courts.*

[*Matt. xxii.* 23-27, 33-46 ; *xxii.* 15-46 ; *xxiii.*
Luke xx. xxi. 1-4.]

27. walking in the temple, i.e. in one of the colonnades
of the court of the Gentiles : cf. John x. 23 ; Acts v. 12.   Here

[1] Latham, *Pastor Pastorum,* 95-98.   See also Swete's notes on the
passage.

and the scribes, and the elders ; and they said unto him, 28
By what authority doest thou these things? or who gave
thee this authority to do these things? And Jesus said 29
unto them, I will ask of you one question, and answer me,
and I will tell you by what authority I do these things.
The baptism of John, was it from heaven, or from men? 30
answer me.   And they reasoned with themselves, saying, 31
If we shall say, From heaven ; he will say, Why then did
ye not believe him?   But should we say, From men— 32
they feared the people : for all verily held John to be
a prophet.   And they answered Jesus and say, We know 33
not.   And Jesus saith unto them, Neither tell I you by
what authority I do these things.

And he began to speak unto them in parables.   A man **12**

---

members of the Sanhedrin come to challenge His authority, this
step being the result of their former plottings (*v.* 18).

28.   these things, i.e. the expulsion of the traders, and
generally, His attitude of opposition to the ruling powers, and
His action in teaching without the required license from the
Scribes[1].

30.   The baptism.   Here put for John's mission as a whole.

31.   they reasoned.   Besides the dilemma here described, it
was clear that in acknowledging John's heavenly commission
they would also acknowledge that of Jesus, since the Baptist
himself bore witness to it, and declared his own to be merely the
preparation for it.

32.   a prophet.   The word means lit. 'a mouthpiece,' i.e. of God.
To deny John's commission would make them guilty of blasphemy in the eyes of the people, and so (Luke adds) liable to
stoning.

33.   We know not.   By this answer they, the teachers of the
people, only escape from the dilemma by confessing their ignorance on a matter which it was their *business* to know about.   If
they could not explain John's 'authority,' that of Jesus must also
be beyond their comprehension, and they stood therefore condemned by Him (see end of n. on 22).

XII. 1.   The O.T. frequently compares Israel to a vineyard,
see esp. Ps. lxxx. 8–19, Is. v. 1–7, passages familiar to Christ's
hearers, who would thus at once grasp the meaning of the
parable: cf. 12, and see n. on xi. 22.

[1] Edersheim, *Life*, II. 382.

planted a vineyard, and set a hedge about it, and digged
a pit for the winepress, and built a tower, and let it out to
2 husbandmen, and went into another country.   And at the
season he sent to the husbandmen a servant, that he
might receive from the husbandmen of the fruits of the
3 vineyard.   And they took him, and beat him, and sent him
4 away empty.   And again he sent unto them another servant ; and him they wounded in the head, and handled
5 shamefully.   And he sent another ; and him they killed :
6 and many others ; beating some, and killing some.   He
had yet one, a beloved son : he sent him last unto them,
7 saying, They will reverence my son.   But those husband-

---

a hedge.   Against robbers and wild animals, cf. Ps. xxx. 13.
The 'hedge' of Israel was its strong geographical position [1], and
its possession of the Law.   **digged a pit,** i.e. cut it out of the
rock.

the winepress, the vat into which the grape-juice ran.

a tower, a look-out for the vine-dressers' use.   The landlord stands for God, the tenants ('husbandmen') are the Jewish
rulers [2], the vineyard the privileges (or the privileged nation) of
Israel.   The other details merely add to the picture of the *care*
of God for Israel.

2.   The tenants paid the landlord 'in kind,' out of the produce
of the vineyard.

3–5.   The slaves stand for the O.T. prophets generally : the
details of their ill-treatment show the patience of God, and the
increasing rebelliousness of the nation.   ' Servant of the Lord '
was a familiar O.T. description of a *prophet*.   Cf. Amos iii. 7,
Zech. i. 6, Jer. vii. 25, xxv. 4, etc.

4.   Note the important differences of rendering in A.V. and
R.V. for this verse.

6. beloved.   See n. on i. 11.   The rest of the parable is
prophetic.

last.   A warning to the nation about to reject its final chance.

7.   The tenants imagine that the son being slain, and the landlord having no more messengers to send, they can seize the
vineyard permanently.   So the rulers who slew the prophets
hoped by slaying the Son of God to secure the 'Kingdom,' but
instead of this it was taken from them and given 'unto others.'

---

[1] G. A. Smith, *H. G.* ch. i.
[2] See Trench, *On the Parables*, 203, and note there quoted from F. D.
Maurice.

men said among themselves, This is the heir; come, let
us kill him, and the inheritance shall be ours.   And they 8
took him, and killed him, and cast him forth out of the
vineyard.   What therefore will the lord of the vineyard 9
do? he will come and destroy the husbandmen, and will
give the vineyard unto others.   Have ye not read even 10
this scripture;

> The stone which the builders rejected,
> The same was made the head of the corner:
> This was from the Lord,   11
> And it is marvellous in our eyes?

And they sought to lay hold on him; and they feared the 12
multitude; for they perceived that he spake the parable
against them: and they left him, and went away.

And they send unto him certain of the Pharisees and 13
of the Herodians, that they might catch him in talk.   And 14

---

8. cast him forth, as the Jews rejected Jesus, denying His
claims, and handing Him over to the Gentiles (Romans) for
punishment.

9. he will come.   The tenants had blindly ignored this
possibility.   According to Matt. the bystanders supply this
climax, while Luke adds that they cried out 'God forbid' on
hearing these words.   The 'coming of the Lord' was a familiar
O.T. phrase, and implies *for judgment*.   The fall of Jerusalem
and annihilation of the Jewish nation fulfilled these words.

10.   A new metaphor now conveys the same lesson.   Jesus
calls himself a rejected stone (Ps. cxviii. 22, 23), the builders
in this case being the Jewish rulers.   (In the Psalm itself the
'stone' is Israel, the 'builders' are foreign enemies.   Here
Christ is the *representative* of Israel.)   This parable goes a step
further than the last, for it shows the triumph of the rejected
'heir.'   Luke adds (xx. 18) that the 'stone' is their final ruin.

even this scripture.   Ironically asked, for they all knew it as
part of the greeting to the Passover pilgrims.   See xi. 9.

the head of the corner, i.e. the stone which holds together
two adjoining walls.   Peter repeats the metaphor (1 Pet. ii.
4–7; Acts iv. 11).   So also does St Paul (Eph. ii. 20), who also
refers to Is. xxviii. 16.

12. they, i.e. such Scribes and chief priests as were present.

13. Herodians.   Practically nothing is known of these 'par-
tisans of Herod,' but they would be naturally hostile to the

when they were come, they say unto him, Master, we know that thou art true, and carest not for any one : for thou regardest not the person of men, but of a truth teachest the way of God : Is it lawful to give tribute unto Cæsar,

15 or not? Shall we give, or shall we not give? But he, knowing their hypocrisy, said unto them, Why tempt ye

16 me? bring me a penny, that I may see it. And they brought it. And he saith unto them, Whose is this image and superscription? And they said unto him, Cæsar's.

17 And Jesus said unto them, Render unto Cæsar the things

Pharisees, who hated all foreign rule. Probably these were Galileans, as Jerusalem was directly governed by a Roman official. Herod was in the city at this time (Luke xxiii. 7). See n. on iii. 6.

14. they say. The flattering words yet betray the impression of sincerity made by Jesus. They felt He would not fear to attack the Roman authority any more than He had feared the Jewish rulers.

the way of God, i.e. the way in which He wishes men to walk.

Is it lawful. A trap set to catch Jesus, for if He said 'no,' the Romans would arrest Him (cf. Luke xxiii. 2); if He said 'yes,' He would become unpopular, and they could safely attack Him.

tribute. A poll-tax paid direct to the emperor's treasury, and hated specially by the Jews, because it proved their subjection to a foreign power, and also because the coin demanded bore the emperor's head, which was considered by them idolatrous.

Cæsar, i.e. Tiberius, who came to the throne A.D. 14.

15. their hypocrisy, in professing to be genuine enquirers. See Luke xx. 20 for details of their plot.

bring me. Only Jewish money was used in the Temple courts.

a penny. A *denarius*, or silver coin equivalent to about half-a-crown of our money. See vi. 37.

16. superscription. The Latin words were TI · CAESAR · DIVI · AVG · F · AVG.

17. The coin proved the emperor's authority over Judaea, while loyalty to the 'powers that be' is not disloyalty to God. Cf. Rom. xiii. 1. Christ's religion was not to be revolutionary, nor was His Church to set itself against the Roman empire.

Render, i.e. ' pay' as a due, rather than 'give,' the word used in 14.

that are Cæsar's, and unto God the things that are God's.
And they marvelled greatly at him.

And there come unto him Sadducees, which say that 18
there is no resurrection; and they asked him, saying, 19
Master, Moses wrote unto us, If a man's brother die, 19
and leave a wife behind him, and leave no child, that his
brother should take his wife, and raise up seed unto his
brother. There were seven brethren: and the first took a 20
wife, and dying left no seed; and the second took her, and 21
died, leaving no seed behind him; and the third likewise:
and the seven left no seed. Last of all the woman also 22
died. In the resurrection whose wife shall she be of 23
them? for the seven had her to wife. Jesus said unto 24
them, Is it not for this cause that ye err, that ye know not
the scriptures, nor the power of God? For when they 25

---

marvelled greatly, because His reply showed tact and wisdom,
while it was also perfectly straightforward.

18. The next question is theological, as the last had been
political.

Sadducees. See n. on viii. **15.** The name is derived from
Zadok, high-priest under Solomon (cf. 1 Kgs i. 32-45). At this
time the sect were chiefly priests (see Acts v. 17), especially in-
fluential at Jerusalem. They were strongly opposed to the
Pharisees, and would know that Jesus also was no friend of that
sect.

19. Moses wrote. See Deut. xxv. 5 foll., which gives this
'levirate law' in full. Its object was to preserve the elder
brother's line, and it made provision for the widows. See
instances of its usage in Gen. xxxviii. and Ruth iv.

20-23. The story was probably a fiction, but was told as
a *possible* case, in order to make a fair test, as it was just con-
ceivable.

22. As *all* the brothers were childless, no one of them could
claim the wife on account of her having borne him children.

24. Jesus' answer is twofold :—the Sadducees' mistake is
due to (1) misunderstanding the very books they quote, which
tacitly imply the resurrection; (2) under-estimating the power of
God, Who can make more than one kind of world. (1) is explained by 26, (2) by 25.

25. (*Ignorance of the power of God.*) **they**, i.e. men generally.
The lesson is that life in the next world is not a mere repetition

shall rise from the dead, they neither marry, nor are given
26 in marriage; but are as angels in heaven.   But as touching the dead, that they are raised; have ye not read in
the book of Moses, in *the place concerning* the Bush, how
God spake unto him, saying, I *am* the God of Abraham,
27 and the God of Isaac, and the God of Jacob? He is not
the God of the dead, but of the living : ye do greatly err.
28   And one of the scribes came, and heard them questioning together, and knowing that he had answered them
well, asked him, What commandment is the first of all?
29 Jesus answered, The first is, Hear, O Israel; The Lord

---

of our present life: its conditions are wholly different.   The
Sadducees were wrong in thinking that a believer in the resurrection must also assume these conditions to be identical, as the
Pharisees did [1]. Cf. S. Paul's teaching on the subject, 1 Cor. xv.
35 foll.

angels, whose very existence the Sadducees denied.

26. (*Ignorance of the Scriptures.*) The point is that long after
the death of the Patriarchs, God spoke of Himself as "the God
of Abraham, Isaac, and Jacob," in a way which showed that His
relation to them was intimate and *permanent*, an idea which
implied the doctrine of a resurrection, since it proved that God's
care for men continued beyond their earthly life.   Such a belief
grew up slowly and gradually, and was still but vague when
Christ came and gave it form and definiteness.

the book of Moses, i.e. the Pentateuch, which bore his name,
and the authority of which was acknowledged by the Sadducees,
who held lax views about the inspiration of the Prophets.

the Bush, a title for one section of the Pentateuch (Ex. iii.)
which was a synagogue 'lesson.'   The division of the Bible
into chapters and verses is modern; the chapters we owe to
Stephen Langton (time of King John) and the verses to a Greek
Testament of 1551.   The R.V. restored the division into paragraphs [2].

27.   greatly err.   The Sadducees were mistaken, but not
hypocritical.

28.   This questioner, according to Mark's account, seems
sincere, but see Matt. xxii. 34.   If he was a Pharisee he must
have been delighted at the Sadducees' discomfiture.

29, 30.   Jesus quotes from Deut. vi. 4 and Lev. xix. 18.   The
first text was written on the Scribes' 'phylacteries,' and was

    [1] Edersheim, *Life*, II. 398, 399.
    [2] Kenyon, *Our Bible and the Ancient Manuscripts*, 186, 225.

our God, the Lord is one: and thou shalt love the Lord 30
thy God with all thy heart, and with all thy soul, and with
all thy mind, and with all thy strength. The second is 31
this, Thou shalt love thy neighbour as thyself. There is
none other commandment greater than these. And the 32
scribe said unto him, Of a truth, Master, thou hast well
said that he is one; and there is none other but he: and 33
to love him with all the heart, and with all the understanding, and with all the strength, and to love his neighbour as himself, is much more than all whole burnt
offerings and sacrifices. And when Jesus saw that he 34
answered discreetly, he said unto him, Thou art not far
from the kingdom of God. And no man after that durst
ask him any question.

And Jesus answered and said, as he taught in the 35
temple, How say the scribes that the Christ is the son of
David? David himself said in the Holy Spirit,   36

---

recited daily by every Jew; it was therefore familiar as a *summary* of the Law, and Jesus taught that the *principle* of Love to
God (the spirit of this summary) includes all particular rules,
and that the *motive* of action is what really matters. Cf. x. 21.

30. heart...soul...mind...strength, a summary of man's
whole being.

31. The second. The answer goes beyond the question, and
shows that love to God and love to man are inseparable.
S. Paul repeats this teaching, Rom. xiii. 9.

thy neighbour. For us the word is explained by the parable
of the Good Samaritan. Luke x. 29-37.

32, 33. The Scribe evidently believed the noble but often
neglected lesson of the Prophets that "to obey is better than
sacrifice." Cf. 1 Sam. xv. 22; Ps. li. 16. According to Matt.
(xxii. 40) Jesus added that all the teaching of the O.T. hung on
these two commandments.

34. discreetly, i.e. he had supplied the reason *why* Jesus had
quoted those two commandments.

not far from, i.e. 'nearly fit to become a subject of' the
Kingdom. There was evidently still some defect in his faith or
practice.

35. answered, by putting a question to His assailants.

the Christ, i.e. the expected Messiah. See n. on i. 1. Jesus
quotes from Ps. cx., which the Jews understood to refer to the

The Lord said unto my Lord,

Sit thou on my right hand,

Till I make thine enemies the footstool of thy feet.

37 David himself calleth him Lord; and whence is he his son? And the common people heard him gladly.

38 And in his teaching he said, Beware of the scribes, which desire to walk in long robes, and *to have* salutations

39 in the marketplaces, and chief seats in the synagogues,

40 and chief places at feasts: they which devour widows' houses, and for a pretence make long prayers; these shall receive greater condemnation.

41 And he sat down over against the treasury, and beheld how the multitude cast money into the treasury: and

42 many that were rich cast in much. And there came

Messiah, and asks them how He could be *descended* from David (cf. Is. xi. 1, and Mark x. 47, xi. 10) and yet be acknowledged by his own ancestor as 'lord.' The only answer could be that David's Son is *divine*. The Jews by their very use of the title 'Son of David' showed their imperfect idea of the Messiah's claims, believing He would merely be a great king on earth. Jesus accepts the common belief of His time that Ps. cx. was written by David. It is now assigned to a later writer.

36. on my right hand, the place of honour at an Eastern court.

37. the common people, opposed to the 'professional' classes of *vv.* 13, 18, 28.

38. in his teaching, i.e. a specimen is given of His warnings to the people against their teachers.

salutations, such as 'Hail, Rabbi,' or 'Abba' (='Father').

39. chief places. In the synagogues a bench facing the people was reserved for distinguished persons.

40. devour widows' houses. Either the Scribes abused the benevolence of rich and pious widows, or perhaps they were dishonest 'trustees' for them.

for a pretence, i.e. of superior piety. See Matt. vi. 5.

greater condemnation, i.e. a severer judgment because they were the guides of the people.

41. Jesus now passes from the Court of the Gentiles to that of the Women.

the treasury, thirteen chests under a colonnade (John viii. 20), each to hold offerings for a different purpose. (Cf. 2 Kings xii. 9.)

a poor widow, and she cast in two mites, which make
a farthing. And he called unto him his disciples, and 43
said unto them, Verily I say unto you, This poor widow
cast in more than all they which are casting into the treasury: for they all did cast in of their superfluity; but she 44
of her want did cast in all that she had, *even* all her
living.

> (*e*).   3rd day (*continued*) : (iii) *from the Temple to the*
> *Mount of Olives.*

And as he went forth out of the temple, one of his **13**
disciples saith unto him, Master, behold, what manner of
stones and what manner of buildings! And Jesus said 2
unto him, Seest thou these great buildings? there shall

---

42. a farthing, the smallest Roman coin, in value about ⅟d.
and said not to be current out of Italy.   If so, Mark here
gives for his Roman readers the Latin equivalent of a Jewish
coin.

43. Jesus here explains the nature of true liberality and again
points out that it is the *motive* of an action which counts (cf. 30
and 2 Cor. viii. 12): Aristotle taught the same lesson, saying
"He who gives a smaller sum, if it be from a smaller store, may
well be the more liberal."

> (*e*).   3rd day (*continued*): (iii) *from the Temple to the*
> *Mount of Olives.*
>
> [*Matt. xxiv.   Luke xxi.* 5–36.]

XIII. 1. as he went forth, viz. on the way back to Bethany
for the night.   We learn from Matt. (xxiii. 38) that He had
just spoken of the ruin which was to befall the Temple.   It was
built of huge blocks of stone, and filled with rich votive offerings.
The Jews believed that Jerusalem could not be taken so long as
Herod's Temple stood, therefore the lament of Jesus over the
coming fall of the city (Luke xix. 41–44) had probably aroused
fear in the disciples as to the safety of the Temple.   (Cf. also
John ii. 19.)

2. great buildings. The Temple area was surrounded by
magnificent colonnades, within which were various courts leading
up to the Sanctuary.   The prophecy was fulfilled 40 years later,
when Titus destroyed Jerusalem in A.D. 70, after a long siege,
graphically described by the Jewish historian Josephus[1].   The

---

[1] A good popular account in Collier's *Great Events of History*, ch. ii.

not be left here one stone upon another, which shall not
be thrown down.

3 And as he sat on the mount of Olives over against
the temple, Peter and James and John and Andrew asked
4 him privately, Tell us, when shall these things be? and
what *shall be* the sign when these things are all about to
5 be accomplished? And Jesus began to say unto them,
6 Take heed that no man lead you astray. Many shall
come in my name, saying, I am *he*; and shall lead many
7 astray. And when ye shall hear of wars and rumours of
wars, be not troubled: *these things* must needs come to

Romans set fire to the Temple, and Titus then gave orders 'to
dig down the whole city and the Temple.' Josephus says that
the site looked afterwards as though it had never been inhabited.
The charge brought against Jesus (xiv. 58) was perhaps founded
on these words, and the saying recorded in John ii. 19. See
also Luke xix. 41–44.

3. as he sat, i.e. in the attitude of a Teacher, as He had sat
to deliver the Sermon on the Mount (Matt. v. 1). He here
speaks in the tone and style of an ancient Prophet, like John the
Baptist before Him, and the author of the Revelation after
Him. His language is based on that of O.T. Prophets, especially
of the two Isaiahs, and is 'apocalyptic' in form, like the Book of
Daniel, e.g. He speaks of the coming judgment on Jerusalem,
and the passing of the old Jewish order before the setting up of
Christ's Kingdom. But this judgment and coming were the
type of other and later events of the same nature (e.g. the Last
Judgment and 'end of the world'), and the prophecy may refer
secondarily to these.

the mount of Olives. n. on xi. 1.

4. Question (1), as to the *time* of fulfilment, is answered
in 5–29, question (2), as to the *sign* of His approach, in 30–32.

5. began to say. The phrase introduces an important
discourse.

6. I am he, i.e. 'the Messiah.' Cf. John viii. 24. See the
account of Simon Magus in Acts viii. 9. Josephus mentions
other impostors before the Fall of Jerusalem.

7. be not troubled, i.e. 'go on quietly with your work.'
There were many disturbances in Palestine before the final
crash came.

7, 8. Partly quoted from Dan. ii. 28; Is. xix. 2. The
language is 'apocalyptic' (see n. on 3) and the details of the

pass; but the end is not yet. For nation shall rise 8 against nation, and kingdom against kingdom: there shall be earthquakes in divers places; there shall be famines: these things are the beginning of travail.

But take ye heed to yourselves: for they shall deliver 9 you up to councils; and in synagogues shall ye be beaten; and before governors and kings shall ye stand for my sake, for a testimony unto them. And the gospel must 10 first be preached unto all the nations. And when they 11 lead you *to judgement*, and deliver you up, be not anxious beforehand what ye shall speak: but whatsoever shall be given you in that hour, that speak ye: for it is not ye that speak, but the Holy Ghost. And brother shall deliver up 12

---

predictions were not therefore literally fulfilled. (See however Acts xi. 28.)

8. travail. Because the sufferings of the Jewish nation in its fall would lead to the birth of a new age.

9. yourselves, i.e. the apostles. **councils**, local law-courts. **synagogues.** See n. on i. 21.

beaten. As were the old Prophets, cf. xii. 3–5. Cf. Paul's record (2 Cor. xi. 24) of 5 scourgings, and see Acts v. 40. Peter and John were brought before the great Council of Jerusalem, Acts iv. 5.

governors. The Gk word was used of the *procurator* of Judæa, e.g. Felix, before whom Paul was brought (Acts xxiii. 24), but may be used of *any* local authority.

kings, e.g. Paul's appearance before Agrippa (Acts xxvi.) and the persecution under Nero, in which S. Peter and S. Paul are said to have suffered martyrdom.

unto them, i.e. their enemies. "The blood of martyrs is the seed of the Church." Note on vi. 11.

10. all the nations. Not to be taken literally: the Gospel had however been 'proclaimed' in nearly every province of the Roman empire before the Fall of Jerusalem.

11. Cf. the similar command given earlier to the apostles (Matt. x. 17–19) and the same prediction (i.e. of *v.* 9) then made. (Possibly Matt. attached the prophetic words to the wrong occasion.)

12. Prophetic language (partly from Micah vii. 6) to describe the loosening of family-ties in the days of the early Christians, when some in a family would remain non-Christian. Judas the traitor must have listened to this prophecy of treachery.

brother to death, and the father his child; and children
shall rise up against parents, and cause them to be put to
13 death.   And ye shall be hated of all men for my name's
sake: but he that endureth to the end, the same shall be
saved.

14   But when ye see the abomination of desolation standing
where he ought not (let him that readeth understand),
then let them that are in Judæa flee unto the mountains :
15 and let him that is on the housetop not go down, nor

---

cause...to be put to death.   Only the Roman authority could
actually inflict capital punishment.

13.   hated of all men.   It is certain that the early Christians
were hated to an extraordinary degree, although they were quiet
and loyal citizens.

to the end = 'even to death.'   A paradox like "He that
will save his life shall lose it," etc. (viii. 35).

14.   A partial answer to the disciples' request for a 'sign.'

the abomination of desolation.   The word translated 'abomination' is a common O.T. term for an idol, or any heathen symbol.   The phrase means 'the defilement which causes desolation,'
and is taken from Daniel (see Dan. ix. 27), where it refers to
the desecration of the Temple by Antiochus Epiphanes.   (Note
the omission by the R.V. of the words " spoken of by Daniel the
Prophet.')   James, the Lord's brother, was murdered in the Temple
courts before the siege of Jerusalem, and this desecration fulfilled
these words of prophecy, and recalled those other words of Jesus
recorded in Luke xiii. 34, 35.

let him that readeth understand.   Perhaps this is a note of
the writer to call attention to this sentence, written when the
fall of the city was at hand [1].   Or the phrase ' him that readeth '
may be a technical term for 'a student of Scripture.'   If so the
words are an appeal from Jesus to such an one to consider the
meaning of Daniel's prophecy [2].

them that are in Judæa, i.e. such Christians as remained
there when the siege began.   They fled to Pella, across the
Jordan.   Possibly ' to flee to the mountain' was a proverbial
phrase, taken from Gen. xix. 17.

15.   on the housetop.   The Oriental sleeping-place, and used
also in the day-time as the natural place to sit.

not go down, i.e. through the house, but rather by an outside
staircase.   (Cf. ii. 4.)

[1] Sanday, *On Inspiration*, 291–293.
[2] Hort, *Lectures on Romans and Ephesians*, 150, 151, note on Eph. iii. 4.

enter in, to take anything out of his house: and let him 16
that is in the field not return back to take his cloke. But 17
woe unto them that are with child and to them that give
suck in those days! And pray ye that it be not in the 18
winter. For those days shall be tribulation, such as there 19
hath not been the like from the beginning of the creation
which God created until now, and never shall be. And 20
except the Lord had shortened the days, no flesh would
have been saved: but for the elect's sake, whom he chose,
he shortened the days. And then if any man shall say 21
unto you, Lo, here is the Christ; or, Lo, there; believe *it*
not: for there shall arise false Christs and false prophets, 22
and shall shew signs and wonders, that they may lead
astray, if possible, the elect. But take ye heed: behold, I 23
have told you all things beforehand.

But in those days, after that tribulation, the sun shall be 24
darkened, and the moon shall not give her light, and the 25
stars shall be falling from heaven, and the powers that are

---

16. his cloke, the upper garment, taken off for work in the fields.

17. woe. This word is frequent in 'apocalyptic' warnings. Cf. Rev. ix. 12, etc.: so also is the phrase 'in those days.' Cf. Zeph. i. 9, 10.

19. Adapted from Dan. xii. 1. The siege lasted 5 months.

20. the elect. This title of the 'chosen nation' is now transferred to the Church of Christ, or the faithful members of it.

21, 22. The Christians would think that the Fall of Jerusalem was the expected final Coming of Christ, and impostors would take advantage of this expectation. **22** is partly from Deut. xiii. 1.

wonders, i.e. 'portents.' **signs** = here, 'miracles.'

23. I have told you, i.e. 'I have warned you against impostors.'

24. See n. on *v.* 3. **in those days**, i.e. in the period which will *begin* with the Fall of Jerusalem. Jesus does not know the moment in that period when He will come. (32.)

24, 25. These portents are taken from Is. xiii. 10, xxxiv. 4; Ezek. xxxii. 7, etc., prophecies which foretell the doom of Jerusalem's enemies. The language is figurative, and not to be taken literally.

26 in the heavens shall be shaken. And then shall they **see**
the Son of man coming in clouds with great power and
27 glory. And then shall he send forth the angels, and shall
gather together his elect from the four winds, from the
uttermost part of the earth to the uttermost part of
heaven.

28 Now from the fig tree learn her parable: when her
branch is now become tender, and putteth forth its leaves,
29 ye know that the summer is nigh; even so ye also, when
ye see these things coming to pass, know ye that he is
30 nigh, *even* at the doors. Verily I say unto you, This
generation shall not pass away, until all these things be
31 accomplished. Heaven and earth shall pass away: but
32 my words shall not pass away. But of that day or that
hour knoweth no one, not even the angels in heaven,
33 neither the Son, but the Father. Take ye heed, watch

---

26. the Son of man. From Dan. vii. 13: see n. on ii. 10.
The original passage (in Dan.) prophesies the downfall of
heathen empires, and the rise of an ideal kingdom on their
ruins. Christ applies the words to Himself, predicting the foun-
dation of His Kingdom on the scattered empires of the world.

27. gather together his elect. A reminiscence of O.T.
passages about the reassembling of the tribes after the Captivity
(cf. Zech. ii. 6; Deut. xxx. 4), here used by Jesus as the type of
the gathering of His new subjects into the Kingdom of Heaven,
and the spread of the Gospel after the destruction of Judaism.

28. her parable. (Cf. xi. 13, 20–25.) The leaves appear at
the Passover season, and probably Jesus points out a fig-tree
near by.

29. these things, i.e. the signs just described (24–27), will
show that the Coming of Christ is at hand.

he = probably 'the Lord.' Cf. Phil. iv. 5.

30. Now begins the answer to the disciples' *first* question:
n. on 4.

this generation, i.e. men now living, therefore the reference
must be to the fall of Jerusalem, and the establishment of the
Church.

32. of that day, i.e. the *precise* date of the events predicted:
in its fullest sense the Coming of Christ, the perfect establishment of His Kingdom, is still in the far future.

neither the Son. An apparent contradiction of John v. 20.
Jesus as *man* was subject to human limitations.

and pray: for ye know not when the time is. *It is* as 34 *when* a man, sojourning in another country, having left his house, and given authority to his servants, to each one his work, commanded also the porter to watch. Watch 35 therefore: for ye know not when the lord of the house cometh, whether at even, or at midnight, or at cockcrowing, or in the morning; lest coming suddenly he find you 36 sleeping. And what I say unto you I say unto all, Watch. 37

(*f*). *4th day: at Jerusalem and Bethany (the anointing).*

Now after two days was *the feast of* the passover and **14** the unleavened bread: and the chief priests and the scribes sought how they might take him with subtilty, and kill him: for they said, Not during the feast, lest haply 2 there shall be a tumult of the people.

---

34. A condensed parable, in which the Son of man is compared to a man going away into foreign lands, the time of his return being quite uncertain.

the porter. He may be taken to stand for the apostles, left in charge of the **servants**, i.e. Christ's followers.

35. The four 'watches' of the night are here enumerated: n. on vi. 45. In the Temple a priest went round the guards every night, choosing his own time: severe punishment was inflicted on any guard found asleep[1].

36. find you sleeping. The Master found His hearers two days later (xiv. 37) literally asleep.

37. unto you (the 'porter,' i.e. the apostles), **unto all** (the 'servants,' i.e. His followers generally). This practical conclusion is in striking contrast with the current Jewish ideas as to the 'coming in Judgment' of the Messiah[2].

(*f*). *4th day: at Jerusalem and Bethany (the anointing).*
[*Matt. xxvi.* 1-16. *Luke xxii.* 1-6. *John xii.* 1-11.]

XIV. 1. the unleavened bread, i.e. the week following the Passover, during which the unleavened bread was still eaten (cf. Exod. xxxiv. 18).

after two days, *inclusive* reckoning. The eve of the Passover had come. This was the meeting of the Sanhedrin (n. viii. 31) which Matt. says took place in the house of Caiaphas (see John xi. 49-52).

[1] Edersheim, *The Temple*, 120.
[2] Edersheim, *Life*, II. bk v. ch. vi.

3 And while he was in Bethany in the house of Simon
the leper, as he sat at meat, there came a woman having
an alabaster cruse of ointment of spikenard very costly;
and she brake the cruse, and poured it over his head.
4 But there were some that had indignation among themselves, *saying*, To what purpose hath this waste of the
5 ointment been made? For this ointment might have
been sold for above three hundred pence, and given to the
6 poor. And they murmured against her. But Jesus said,
Let her alone; why trouble ye her? she hath wrought
7 a good work on me. For ye have the poor always with
you, and whensoever ye will ye can do them good: but
8 me ye have not always. She hath done what she could :
she hath anointed my body aforehand for the burying.
9 And verily I say unto you, Wheresoever the gospel shall

3–9. John places the anointing *before* the last week, and
perhaps Matt. and Mark record it here because it supplies
the motive for Judas's action (see 10). The anointing by the
'sinner' described by Luke (vii. 36–50) is a quite distinct
incident, though both took place in the house of a Simon ; but
this was a common Jewish name. The woman *here* is Mary, the
sister of Martha and Lazarus.

3. Simon the leper. Possibly he had been cured; he was
apparently not present.

alabaster...spikenard. See R.V. margin. **cruse**=a small
bottle. Cf. A.V.

she brake, i.e. knocked the head off, so that it could not be
used again.

4. some. It was Judas Iscariot according to John (n. on 10).

5. three hundred pence. A 'penny' (*denarius*) was a
workman's daily wage at that time (Matt. xx. 2). Note on vi. 37.

6. Jesus points out that the *motive* of the deed is what
matters. The magnificence and costliness of cathedrals (far
beyond the practical needs of those who use them) is thus
justified : cf. Wordsworth's *Sonnet on King's College Chapel.*

7. me ye have not always. Jesus now claims for Himself
acts of homage, and so impresses on the disciples His Kingship.

8. for the burying. Jesus does not imply that she *knew*
that He was about to die, but He accepts her act as a final
service, and a recognition of His dignity. She *may* have known
from His own predictions what was to happen.

be preached throughout the whole world, that also which
this woman hath done shall be spoken of for a memorial
of her.

And Judas Iscariot, he that was one of the twelve, went 10
away unto the chief priests, that he might deliver him unto them. And they, when they heard it, were glad, and 11
promised to give him money. And he sought how he
might conveniently deliver him *unto them.*

(*g*). *5th day : at Jerusalem :* (i) *the Passover Feast.*

And on the first day of unleavened bread, when they 12
sacrificed the passover, his disciples say unto him, Where
wilt thou that we go and make ready that thou mayest
eat the passover? And he sendeth two of his disciples, 13

---

9. throughout the whole world. Notice the *importance*
claimed by Jesus for His teaching.

10. Judas Iscariot. Only mentioned hitherto in the list of
the Twelve (iii. 19). Regarding **3-9** as a digression, and
looking back to **2**, we see that the arrival of Judas evidently
gave the priests the chance they were waiting for. The
motives for his act are not given at all by Mark, who possibly
placed here the account of Mary's devotion to mark the contrast
with Judas's treachery.

11. money. Matt. gives the exact sum (xxvi. 15).

conveniently, i.e. without a riot and interference from the
people.

(*g*). *5th day : at Jerusalem :* (i) *the Passover Feast.*

[*Matt. xxvi.* 17-36. *Luke xxii.* 7-40. *John xiii.* 1-38,
xviii. 1, 2.]

12. the first day, etc., the 14th of Nisan, when the lamb was
killed (see n. on 1), and the unleavened bread was first eaten.

they = the Jews, **sacrificed,** i.e. 'were wont to slay.' The
lamb was killed in the Priests' court of the Temple.

the passover, i.e. the lamb: cf. **1,** where the sense of the
phrase is wider.

make ready, i.e. buy the lamb and other necessary things.
Jesus and His disciples share the feast as one family.

13. two. Peter and John, according to Luke. Possibly the
owner of the house supplied the lamb. See xii. 4.

and saith unto them, Go into the city, and there shall
meet you a man bearing a pitcher of water : follow him ;
14 and wheresoever he shall enter in, say to the goodman of
the house, The Master saith, Where is my guest-chamber,
15 where I shall eat the passover with my disciples ? And
he will himself shew you a large upper room furnished
16 *and* ready : and there make ready for us. And the disciples went forth, and came into the city, and found as he
had said unto them : and they made ready the passover.
17   And when it was evening he cometh with the twelve.
18 And as they sat and were eating, Jesus said, Verily I say

---

into the city, i.e. from Bethany. **a man**, a servant belonging
to the 'goodman.' Tradition says it was Mark himself.

14. the Master. Evidently the 'goodman' was a follower
of Jesus.

my guest-chamber. Again He claims service as a right
(n. on 7).

15. furnished—either with couches to recline on, or with
carpets.

16. This *v.* implies that here (as when He sent for the ass's
colt, xi. 1) Jesus had superhuman knowledge of ordinary things:
at an earlier period the signs of such power were rare.

made ready. The chief ceremonies were, Four cups of
wine, taken at stated intervals ; the eating of bitter herbs and
unleavened bread, with the explanation of the meaning of the
ceremony ; the singing of the Hallel (Ps. cxiii.–cxviii.) in two
portions ; the eating of the lamb [1].

17. evening. The lambs were not slain till after the
evening sacrifice. But the feast was not at this period always
celebrated at night, and some of the old customs had been
dropped, e.g. they did not now eat the meal *standing*, nor
in travelling dress. (Cf. Exod. xii. 11.) **cometh**, i.e. from
Bethany to Jerusalem.

18. sat. R.V. marg. 'reclined,' i.e. on a couch, two or
three together. From John xiii. 23, 24, it seems that Jesus,
between Peter and John, occupied one couch, and presided over
the feast.

were eating, i.e. the bread and herbs (the first course) had
been served, and the first cup had been blessed and drunk. First
of all Jesus had washed the disciples' feet (John xiii. 3 foll.).

---

[1] Edersheim, *Life*, ii. bk v. chs. x., xi. Hastings' *Dict. of the Bible*, ii.
634.

unto you, One of you shall betray me, *even* he that eateth
with me. They began to be sorrowful, and to say unto 19
him one by one, Is it I? And he said unto them, *It is* 20
one of the twelve, he that dippeth with me in the dish.
For the Son of man goeth, even as it is written of him: 21
but woe unto that man through whom the Son of man is
betrayed! good were it for that man if he had not been
born.

And as they were eating, he took bread, and when he 22

---

one of you. The prediction of betrayal had not before been
brought home to the disciples, who can hardly have suspected
Judas. The writers of the Gospels always allude to him as the
traitor, but they wrote of course after the event.

he that eateth with me, quoted from Ps. xli. 9. Cf. John xiii.
18. Such treachery would be a breach of the universal Oriental
law of hospitality.

19. one by one. In the Oberammergau Passion Play the
question is asked by each of the Twelve in turn. (Cf. also the
repetition in Bach's Passion music, St Matthew.)

20. The manner of the answer is given in detail in John's
account (xiii. 23—26).

the dish. Probably the '*charoseth*,' or sauce, into which the
president of the feast dipped the bread and herbs before handing
them round. John's phrase "he...for whom I shall dip the sop"
is clearer than Mark's rendering. The latter lays stress on the
'dipping together,' i.e. the sharing of the dish, to mark the
heinousness of the treachery (see n. on 18).

21. even as it is written, e.g. in Is. liii. (the sufferings of
'the Servant.')

but woe unto that man, i.e. the traitor's act is none the less
black because he is (unconsciously) working out the purpose of
God.

good were it etc. (cf. ix. 42). The Rabbis used such ex-
pressions for hopeless vileness.

22. as they were eating. The Feast had now reached its
third stage; the first part of the Hallel (Ps. cxiii. cxiv.) had been
sung, and the President now ate bread and herbs: the eating of
the lamb came later. The Blessing and Breaking of the bread
were probably part of the usual ritual, but Jesus gives a new
meaning to the rite by adding the words "This is my Body." In
the discourse on the Bread of Life, after the feeding of the 5000
(John vi. 48—58, and see n. on vi. 41), Jesus had prepared for
this teaching. This Feast became in His hands an acted parable,

had blessed, he brake it, and gave to them, and said,
23 Take ye: this is my body. And he took a cup, and when
he had given thanks, he gave to them: and they all drank
24 of it. And he said unto them, This is my blood of the
25 covenant, which is shed for many. Verily I say unto you,
I will no more drink of the fruit of the vine, until that day
when I drink it new in the kingdom of God.
26 And when they had sung a hymn, they went out unto
the mount of Olives.

---

which later the disciples would understand still better, for after
His Death they would see that this special Passover symbolized
a greater deliverance than that of the Exodus, wrought by the
sacrifice of His own Life. The words "This do in remembrance
of me" followed here, as S. Paul alone tells us (1 Cor. xi. 24).
The Gospel accounts (in the best MSS.) give no directions for the
repetition of the ceremony.

23. a cup. Probably the third (see n. on 16) or Cup of
Blessing, now given a new and mystical meaning by Jesus.

24. This is my blood etc. Partly quoted from Ex. xxiv. 8,
which describes how Moses sprinkled the people with the blood
of the sacrifice which ratified the Old Covenant (of the Law)
between God and Israel. The wine symbolizes Christ's blood,
which was to ratify the New Covenant (of the Gospel) between
God and man; cf. S. Paul's account, 1 Cor. xi. 25. Jeremiah
(xxxi. 31–34) had prophesied such a New Covenant, when God's
Law would be in men's *hearts*, and not exist merely as a code of
rules.

shed for many. Matt. (xxvi. 28) adds "for the remission of
sins," showing that the meaning of the phrase is that the blood is
in some way a sin-offering.

25. I will no more drink etc. This mysterious saying apparently means, (1) That He will not partake of another meal
before His death, (2) That hereafter He will share another **Feast**
with His subjects, when His Kingdom is established.

drink it new, i.e. in that Kingdom where all things were to
become 'new' (Rev. xxi. 5); then only will come the complete
fulfilment of these words.

26. sung a hymn, i.e. the second part of the Hallel (Ps. cxv.
–cxviii.) which ended the Feast (n. on 16). Mark, writing for
Gentile readers (see Introd. p. xv.), does not describe the ritual of
the Passover, though we can trace its ceremonies through his
allusions. Jesus observed the great national Feast as a devout
Jew, and gave it a new and deeper meaning. The Paschal *lamb*
is nowhere mentioned: whether it was eaten or not, the disciples

And Jesus saith unto them, All ye shall be offended : 27
for it is written, I will smite the shepherd, and the sheep
shall be scattered abroad. Howbeit, after I am raised up, 28
I will go before you into Galilee. But Peter said unto 29
him, Although all shall be offended, yet will not I. And 30
Jesus saith unto him, Verily I say unto thee, that thou to-
day, *even* this night, before the cock crow twice, shalt
deny me thrice. But he spake exceeding vehemently, I 31
I must die with thee, I will not deny thee. And in like
manner also said they all.

    (*h*).   *5th day (continued)*: (ii) *at Gethsemane.*

And they come unto a place which was named Gethse- 32
mane : and he saith unto his disciples, Sit ye here, while

---

afterwards would see that the President of the Feast was the real
'victim,' of which the lamb was the type. Cf. 1 Cor. v. 7, 8 ;
Heb. vii. 27, x. 10.

they went out, i.e. towards Bethany, as they had done each
evening. The discourses and prayer of John xv.–xvii. were
probably spoken on the way.

27. **shall be offended.** See R.V. marg. 'caused to stumble.'
The words recall His stern warnings to them before, see iv. 17,
ix. 42–50.

it is written. A free adaptation of Zech. xiii. 7, *q.v.*

28. **into Galilee,** whither the disciples would naturally return
after the Passover. Matt. (xxviii. 17) records that He met them
in Galilee, and the appendix to John's Gospel (xxi.) describes
another meeting by the Lake.

29, 30. Peter's vain boast is met with a prediction of denial
as well as of desertion.

to-day, even this night. The Jews reckoned the day to begin
with the preceding sunset : the 6th day had now begun.

twice. A detail found in Mark only (see Introd. p. xxx.). The
first crowing should have recalled him to himself.

31. **die with thee.** John says (xi. 16) that Thomas proposed
this.

    (*h*).   *5th day (continued)*: (ii) *at Gethsemane.*
    [*Matt. xxvi.* 37–46. *Luke xxii.* 41–53. *John xviii.* 1, 2.]

32. **a place,** see R.V. marg. John states that it was a garden
beyond Kidron, and a favourite resort of Jesus. The traditional
site is still pointed out on the Mount of Olives, but is not now
regarded as certainly identified. (See Hastings' *Dict.*)

CH.   7

33 I pray. And he taketh with him Peter and James and
John, and began to be greatly amazed, and sore troubled.
34 And he saith unto them, My soul is exceeding sorrowful
35 even unto death: abide ye here, and watch. And he
went forward a little, and fell on the ground, and prayed
that, if it were possible, the hour might pass away from
36 him. And he said, Abba, Father, all things are possible
unto thee; remove this cup from me: howbeit not what I
37 will, but what thou wilt. And he cometh, and findeth
them sleeping, and saith unto Peter, Simon, sleepest thou?
38 couldest thou not watch one hour? Watch and pray,

---

33. The same three who had been present at the Transfiguration (ix. 2) and probably on other occasions also, accom-
pany Him now: so far there was nothing unusual.

amazed. As if He were 'startled,' now that the crisis had
come, and He realized its terrors, thus showing once more the
reality of His human nature.

34. he saith unto them, having chosen the three to witness
His sufferings, and also craving for sympathy with true human
instinct. The words recall Ps. xlii. 6, 11, xliii. 5.

watch, that they might be witnesses (see last note). Cf. also
xiii. 35, 37.

35. the hour, in the sense of 'the critical hour,' a phrase
familiar in John's Gospel. (John vii. 30, viii. 20, xvii. 1.) He
prayed that He might escape the appointed suffering, if it were
in accordance with the Father's will.

36. Abba. An Aramaic word for 'father.' Either Our Lord
repeated the invocation in both languages, or 'Father' is an
explanatory note of the writer. Possibly the double phrase was
familiar, cf. Rom. viii. 15.

this cup. See n. on x. 38 and the reff. to the Psalms.

what thou wilt. In the spirit of the Lord's Prayer, "Thy
will be done."

37. sleeping. They must have heard *something* of His
prayer (reported on the authority of one of them), but were overcome by sleep during the conflict, of which 36 records only the
beginning.

Simon, a return to the old name used before his call, as if to
suggest that he was no longer a true disciple. Cf. the return to
'Peter' in xvi. 7.

37, 38. watch. They would recall the great discourse of
xiii. and its final exhortation, "What I say unto you, I say unto
all, Watch."

that ye enter not into temptation: the spirit indeed is willing, but the flesh is weak. And again he went away, 39 and prayed, saying the same words. And again he came, 40 and found them sleeping, for their eyes were very heavy; and they wist not what to answer him. And he cometh 41 the third time, and saith unto them, Sleep on now, and take your rest: it is enough; the hour is come; behold, the Son of man is betrayed into the hands of sinners. Arise, let us be going: behold, he that betrayeth me is at 42 hand.

And straightway, while he yet spake, cometh Judas, one 43 of the twelve, and with him a multitude with swords and staves, from the chief priests and the scribes and the elders. Now he that betrayed him had given them 44 a token, saying, Whomsoever I shall kiss, that is he;

---

38. into temptation. Again an echo of the Lord's Prayer (n. on 36).

the spirit...the flesh. The contrast is common in S. John and in the Epistles: e.g. John vi. 63, Gal. v. 17.

41. sleep on now. Said in irony; their opportunity for watching was gone.

it is enough, i.e. reproach is useless now: we must act. With these words the tone suddenly changes: the three were doubtless now aroused.

sinners. The word was used by the Jews for 'outcasts' or 'reprobates': note then its force when applied here to the rulers.

42. let us be going, viz. 'to meet the traitor' (cf. John xviii. 4). The conflict is over and He calmly faces betrayal and death.

he that betrayeth me. The disciples would recall His strange words at the Supper (18–21). From 43 it is clear that Judas's party were not yet in sight. John (xviii. 2) explains how Judas knew the place.

43. one of the twelve. This emphatic description of the traitor shows the impression made on his contemporaries by his deed; cf. 10, 20.

a multitude. Probably of Temple police and Roman soldiers (see John xviii. 3): their arms were not military weapons, but clubs and the short swords worn by ordinary people (cf. Luke xxii. 36–38). The three classes of the Sanhedrin are mentioned (n. on viii. 31), but it is not clear whether the arrest had been *formally* decided on by them.

44. I shall kiss. The ordinary greeting given to a Rabbi.

45 take him, and lead him away safely. And when he was
come, straightway he came to him, and saith, Rabbi ; and
46 kissed him. And they laid hands on him, and took him.
47 But a certain one of them that stood by drew his sword,
and smote the servant of the high priest, and struck off
48 his ear. And Jesus answered and said unto them, Are ye
come out, as against a robber, with swords and staves to
49 seize me? I was daily with you in the temple teaching,
and ye took me not: but *this is done* that the scriptures
50 might be fulfilled. And they all left him, and fled.
51   And a certain young man followed with him, having a
linen cloth cast about him, over *his* naked *body* : and they
52 lay hold on him ; but he left the linen cloth, and fled
naked.

---

safely. Judas would remember how Jesus had escaped on other
occasions.
45.   Mark does not record what Jesus said to Judas; the other
accounts vary considerably, owing no doubt to the confusion and
excitement of the moment.
47. a certain one. Peter, according to John (xviii. 10).
his sword. Cf. the mention of swords in the Garden, Luke
xxii. 38, 49. The other accounts record Jesus' rebuke, and
Luke adds that He healed the man.
48. as against a robber. Their weapons suggested a
struggle with a desperate ruffian. Pilate probably sent soldiers
on hearing the rumour that He was heading a revolt.
49. the scriptures, esp. Is. liii.
50. left him, and fled, fulfilling the prediction of 27. Two of
them followed later at a safe distance, Peter and presumably
John (cf. John xviii. 15).
51. a certain young man. Probably Mark himself (who
alone records the incident) or some friend of his. The man was
well-to-do (he wore 'linen'), and Mark's family owned a house
in Jerusalem (Acts xii. 12, 13), possibly the very house where
the Last Supper took place, and to which Judas may have led
the band, thus rousing from sleep the 'young man,' who showed
by his flight that he was a follower.

(i). 6th day: (1) *the Jewish Trial.*

And they led Jesus away to the high priest: and there 53 come together with him all the chief priests and the elders and the scribes. And Peter had followed him afar 54 off, even within, into the court of the high priest; and he was sitting with the officers, and warming himself in the light *of the fire.* Now the chief priests and the whole 55 council sought witness against Jesus to put him to death;

(i). 6th day: (1) *the Jewish Trial.*

[*Matt. xxvi.* 57-75. *Luke xxii.* 54-62. *John xviii.* 24, 15-27.]

53. the high priest, Caiaphas: John tells us that He was first taken before Annas, the ex-high-priest and father-in-law of Caiaphas. The Romans had deposed Annas, but strict Jews would regard him as still high-priest. The Jewish 'trial' consisted of 3 parts: (1) an informal examination at night, either by Annas or Caiaphas; (2) a more regular 'trial' early next morning before the Sanhedrin, presided over by Caiaphas, with witnesses, the high-priest's 'adjuration,' and the verdict; (3) the formal confirmation of the verdict by the Sanhedrin later in the morning. Mark begins with (2). How far were the proceedings legal according to Jewish law [1]? The trial by *night* was illegal, so was the *hurried* procedure, and the first examination *without witnesses* (this explains Jesus' answers, John xviii. 21-23). Again, the final verdict might only be given at an *adjourned* meeting, at least 12 hours later. The Law made protest against any kind of haste in a trial on a capital charge.

54. The story of Peter's denial 54, and 66-72 (supplied by Peter himself to Mark), is a digression from the main story of the Trial.

the court, with rooms opening into it like a Roman *atrium.* John was known to the high priest (John xviii. 15) and so obtained admission for Peter.

the officers, the Temple police, n. on 43.

warming himself. A touch peculiar to Mark. Jerusalem is nearly 4000 ft. above the sea, and nights in spring would be cold. The fire was a brazier of charcoal. (John xviii. 18.)

in the light of the fire. The blaze in the dark hall made him recognizable. The R.V. brings out this picturesque touch. Cf. with A.V.

55. We now turn to the principal scene, which was going on in one of the rooms opening out of the court. This was probably

[1] For the whole subject of the Trial, see Taylor Innes, *The Trial of Jesus Christ* (T. and T. Clark, 1899).

56 and found it **not**. For many bare false witness against
57 him, and their witness **agreed** not together. And there
   stood up certain, and bare false witness against him, say-
58 ing, We heard him say, I will destroy this temple that is
   made with hands, and in three days I will build another
59 made without hands. And not even so did their witness
60 agree together. And the high priest stood up in the
   midst, and asked Jesus, saying, Answerest thou nothing?

---

the informal meeting (n. on 53). In a Jewish trial there was no
'prosecutor,' but the evidence of two witnesses, *if it agreed*, con-
stituted the charge (see 1 Kgs xxi. 8–13). Here, however, the
Sanhedrin practically *prosecuted*, as they 'sought for' witnesses.
Legally they ought to have assumed the innocence of Jesus till
His guilt was proved.

found it not. Jewish law distinguished three kinds of evidence :
(*a*) a vain testimony (i.e. one which could not be accepted by
itself) ; (*b*) a standing testimony (i.e. one which must be con-
firmed by other evidence); (*c*) an equal testimony (i.e. the
evidence of two witnesses who exactly agreed together).

56–58. Apparently (*a*) 'vain' testimony was first given, and
set aside ; (*b*) then a 'standing' testimony was given in a witness's report of a saying of Jesus : (*c*) this failed to become
'equal' testimony owing to the discrepancy of the other witnesses'
reports.

58. The charge was one of blasphemy against the Temple,
the symbol of God's presence among men. This crime was
regarded by the Jews as treason against the Divine Head of the
nation (cf. Acts vi. 13).

we heard him say. They either distort His words (see John
ii. 19), or are reporting a saying unknown to us. His teaching
did cause the old order, with its Temple and sacrifices, to pass
away. The words may be a perversion of His prophecy of the
fall of the Temple (xiii. 2). See n. on xiii. 1.

I will build another. See John's explanation of the similar
saying (ii. 19–22), but the words may have a deeper meaning
still, referring to the Christian Church, the 'Body of Christ,'
which replaced the old Jewish Church with its Temple and
observances[1]. Cf. Stephen's teaching, Acts vi. 14, vii. 49.

59, 60. According to Jewish law the Prisoner ought here to
have been dismissed (see n. on 56–58). Caiaphas most illegally
puts the Prisoner on His oath (Matt. xxvi. 63) and tries to make
Him give evidence against Himself. From John xviii. 14 we

---

[1] Hort, *The Christian Ecclesia*, 163, 164.

what is it which these witness against thee? But he held 61
his peace, and answered nothing. Again the high priest
asked him, and saith unto him, Art thou the Christ, the
Son of the Blessed? And Jesus said, I am: and ye shall 62
see the Son of man sitting at the right hand of power, and
coming with the clouds of heaven. And the high priest 63
rent his clothes, and saith, What further need have we of
witnesses? Ye have heard the blasphemy: what think 64
ye? And they all condemned him to be worthy of death.
And some began to spit on him, and to cover his face, 65
and to buffet him, and to say unto him, Prophesy: and
the officers received him with blows of their hands.

And as Peter was beneath in the court, there cometh 66
one of the maids of the high priest; and seeing Peter 67
warming himself, she looked upon him, and saith, Thou

---

know that he had decided that Jesus' death was a political
necessity.

61. answered nothing. First Caiaphas tries to make Him
answer the insufficient testimony, an outrageous method of trial.

the Son of the Blessed, i.e. of God, thus avoiding the use of
the Holy name. Caiaphas believed that the Messiah would be
'the Son of God.'

62. I am. A definite assertion, followed by words taken
partly from Dan. vii. 13, claiming the Messiahship, and declaring
that He is about to establish the Messiah's kingdom. The Jews
would recognize the quotation as Messianic. Cf. xiii. 26 for
similar language. This is the climax of the long conflict between
Christ and the rulers. He, the Prisoner on trial, is revealed as
their Judge. Cf. nn. on xi. 22, xii. 10.

63. rent his clothes, lit. ' his tunics.' An action only allowed
to the high-priest when hearing blasphemous words, and not (as
in the case of other men) for private grief (see Lev. x. 6, xxi. 10).
The claim to divinity was 'blasphemy,' and this was treason
against the Divine Ruler of Israel: see n. on 58.

64. condemned him to be worthy of death. The limit of their
powers. Only the Roman authority could *pass* sentence of death.

65. Prophesy, i.e. to prove His Messiahship.

66. beneath. The room of the Trial was approached by
steps from the court.

one of the maids. She who had already let Peter in (John
xviii. 16, 17).

68 also wast with the Nazarene, *even* Jesus.   But he denied,
saying, I neither know, nor understand what thou sayest:
and he went out into the porch; and the cock crew.
69 And the maid saw him, and began again to say to them
70 that stood by, This is *one* of them.   But he again denied
it.   And after a little while again they that stood by said
to Peter, Of a truth thou art *one* of them; for thou art a
71 Galilæan.   But he began to curse, and to swear, I know
72 not this man of whom ye speak.   And straightway the
second time the cock crew.   And Peter called to mind
the word, how that Jesus said unto him, Before the cock
crow twice, thou shalt deny me thrice.   And when he
thought thereon, he wept.

(*j*). *6th day* (*continued*): (ii) *The Roman Trial.*

15   And straightway in the morning the chief priests with
the elders and scribes, and the whole council, held a

---

67. thou also. A hint of the presence of another (John
xviii. 15).

68. he denied, being challenged unexpectedly: if he too had
been put on trial he would probably have stood firm.   Note
the vivid details of this episode, which must have come from
Peter himself.   The impetuous words we may paraphrase, 'I do
not even know what you are talking about.'

porch. A word used here only.   It was probably a small
outer hall leading from the street into the court.

69. the maid. In Matt. the speaker is *another* maid.   Mark's
account puts Peter's conduct at its worst, relating a spontaneous
second denial.

70. a Galilæan. He was betrayed by his guttural pro-
nunciation (Matt. xxvi. 73).

71. to curse, i.e. he called down a curse on himself, if his
words were untrue.

72. the cock crew, a sign of dawn.   Mark (best MS.) does
not mention the first crowing, which must have been unheeded
by Peter in the agitation of the moment.

(*j*). *6th day* (*continued*): (ii) *The Roman Trial.*
[*Matt. xxvii.* 1-26.   *Luke xxiii.* 1-24.   *John xviii.* 28-*xix.* 1]

XV. 1. in the morning, i.e. between dawn and the third hour,
when the Crucifixion took place.   The Greek word used is not
precise.

consultation, and bound Jesus, and carried him away, and delivered him up to Pilate. And Pilate asked him, 2 Art thou the King of the Jews? And he answering saith unto him, Thou sayest. And the chief priests accused 3

---

the whole council. Joseph of Arimathea (Luke xxiii. 51) and Nicodemus (John vii. 50, xix. 39) however held aloof.

a consultation. This was the *formal* meeting of the Sanhedrin, called to confirm the sentence (n. on xiv. 53), and was the last stage of the Jewish Trial, the only one approximately legal in form. It was probably held in the house of Caiaphas. Note how the *priests* took the lead, inducing the other members of the Sanhedrin to agree with them.

bound Jesus. To prevent a rescue by the people.

to Pilate. His official residence was Caesarea Stratonis on the coast, but he was obliged to be in Jerusalem at the Passover season to quell riots among the crowds of pilgrims. For Pilate's office see Introd. p. xxviii. He had a reputation for cruelty (see also Luke xiii. 1) and was eventually recalled on a charge of ill-treatment of the Samaritans, but otherwise he does not seem to have been worse than other Roman provincial governors. He wished, as a Roman would, to do justice to Jesus, but fear of evil tongues (John xix. 12) led him to give way to the Jewish mob. A Roman governor would have small interest in the religious and political ideas of the foreigners he ruled (cf. Gallio and St Paul, Acts xviii. 12–15). Pilate is mentioned in the famous sentence of Tacitus (*Ann.* xv. 44) which records the death of Christ. The *place* of the Roman Trial was either Herod's new palace, used possibly by the procurator during his visits to Jerusalem, or, more probably, the Antonia, a fort on the N. side of the Temple area : see Acts xxi. 37, xxii. 24.

The Jews wished Pilate to confirm and execute their sentence : but he insisted on hearing the case himself, and came out to meet them, as they would not enter 'the palace' for fear of pollution during the Passover. He took Jesus into the palace (*praetorium*, see John xviii. 28–33) and there questioned Him. Note the three stages in this Trial : (*a*) Pilate's interview with the Sanhedrists outside, (*b*) his examination of Jesus in the *praetorium*, (*c*) he brings Him out again to the Sanhedrists. Apparently in front of the *praetorium* a moveable 'tribunal' was set up over a 'pavement': see John xix. 33.

2. The governor asks if the Accused claims to be the Messiah, a king, i.e. a rebel against the Roman authority, guilty of high treason.

thou sayest, i.e. 'It is you that say so, not I.' John (xviii. 33–38) explains that Jesus went on to describe the nature of His kingship, and satisfied Pilate that it was not politically dangerous.

4 him of many things. And Pilate again asked him, saying,
Answerest thou nothing? behold how many things they
5 accuse thee of. But Jesus no more answered anything;
insomuch that Pilate marvelled.

6   Now at the feast he used to release unto them one
7 prisoner, whom they asked of him. And there was one
called Barabbas, *lying* bound with them that had made
insurrection, men who in the insurrection had committed
8 murder. And the multitude went up and began to ask
9 him *to do* as he was wont to do unto them. And Pilate
answered them, saying, Will ye that I release unto you
10 the King of the Jews? For he perceived that for envy
11 the chief priests had delivered him up. But the chief
priests stirred up the multitude, that he should rather
12 release Barabbas unto them. And Pilate again answered
and said unto them, What then shall I do unto him whom
13 ye call the King of the Jews? And they cried out again,
14 Crucify him. And Pilate said unto them, Why, what evil

---

3. accused him. Pilate had now brought Jesus out again,
and declared he could find no fault in Him (Luke xxiii. 4).

many things, e.g. the false charge that He forbade payment
of the tribute-money to the Emperor: Luke xxiii. 2, 5.

5. Again He refused to answer false charges, as at the Jewish
Trial (xiv. 60, 61), though He replied to the *questions* put by
Caiaphas and Pilate.

6. used to release. Such practices at the time of festivals
are mentioned in both Greek and Roman history.

7. one called Barabbas. The phrase shows he was a
notorious person: 'son of Abba,' his first name is not given.

8. went up. This threatening advance of the shouting mob
overcame Pilate's intentions of doing justice, though at first
he hoped to find a way out of his dilemma (9, 10). This hope
was frustrated by the Sanhedrists, who urged the mob to claim
Barabbas, evidently a popular hero.

11. stirred up. The word implies that they moved about
amongst the crowd, arguing and volubly persuading them.

12. Pilate again...said. In the interval before this second
appeal the priests had swayed the fickle mob. Cf. Matt.'s
account (xxvii. 21).

14. Pilate further shows his well-meaning weakness by arguing

hath he done? But they cried out exceedingly, Crucify
him. And Pilate, wishing to content the multitude, 15
released unto them Barabbas, and delivered Jesus, when
he had scourged him, to be crucified.

(*k*). *6th day (continued)*: (iii) *The Death.*

And the soldiers led him away within the court, which 16
is the Prætorium; and they call together the whole band.
And they clothe him with purple, and plaiting a crown of 17
thorns, they put it on him; and they began to salute him, 18

---

with the shouting mob. Matt. (xxvii. 19) records the striking
incident of the message sent by his wife, Claudia Procula.

15. wishing to content. The confession of his timorous
weakness. Now he washed his hands before the mob (Matt.
xxvii. 24) to show that he held the people responsible rather
than himself. Luke (xxiii. 6–12) records that Pilate sent Jesus
to Herod Antipas, tetrarch of Galilee, hearing He was a
Galilean. Pilate avoided passing a regular sentence of death
even now.

scourged. The Roman *flagellum* was made of leather thongs
loaded with pieces of metal. It was usual to scourge a man
condemned to be crucified, and probably Pilate hoped that the
people might be satisfied with this torture (Luke xxiii. 22).
See John's record (xix. 1–16) of Pilate's further attempts to save
Jesus, and the reason for his yielding at length. It is possible
that he wished to hasten death by the scourging.

(*k*). *6th day (continued)*: (iii) *The Death.*
[*Matt. xxvii.* 27–61. *Luke xxiii.* 16–56. *John xix.* 2–42.]

16. the soldiers, i.e. those in attendance on Pilate who were
told off to execute the sentence.

band, lit. the 'cohort,' or 10th part of a legion (i.e. 600 men)
or possibly the 'maniple' (200 men): here it means all the
available men of Pilate's guard.

17. purple. Probably a soldier's scarlet cloak (cf. Matt.
xxvii. 28), suggesting by its colour the robe worn by kings, 'royal
purple.'

a crown. In imitation perhaps of the Emperor's laurel-
wreath.

of thorns. Probably the wild thistle which grew near at hand.

18. Matt. adds the detail of a mock sceptre.

19 Hail, King of the Jews! And they smote his head with
a reed, and did spit upon him, and bowing their knees
20 worshipped him. And when they had mocked him, they
took off from him the purple, and put on him his garments.
And they lead him out to crucify him.

21 And they compel one passing by, Simon of Cyrene,
coming from the country, the father of Alexander and
Rufus, to go *with them*, that he might bear his cross.
22 And they bring him unto the place Golgotha, which is,
23 being interpreted, The place of a skull. And they offered
him wine mingled with myrrh: but he received it not.
24 And they crucify him, and part his garments among them,

Hail. A parody of the familiar greeting to the Emperor. The
soldiers, like Pilate, supposed that Jesus had set Himself up
against Tiberius.

20. lead him out, i.e. 'from the *praetorium*' or 'from the
city.' The place of the Crucifixion, and therefore the route to it,
are still uncertain.

21. compel, the word implies 'forced service,' and is of Persian origin: cf. the S. African 'commandeer.' At first Jesus carried
His own cross (n. on viii. 34), which in pictures is usually
represented as impossibly large and heavy.

from the country. Presumably they met Simon just outside
the city.

Cyrene. A town in the N. of Africa; it contained a Jewish
colony: cf. Acts ii. 10, xiii. 1.

Alexander and Rufus. Mentioned as if well known to the
early readers of Mark. There is a greeting to a Rufus in Rom.
xvi. 13. Both names were common.

22. Golgotha. An Aramaic word meaning a 'skull.' The
same word (in its Heb. form) occurs Judges ix. 53.

Here it is the name given to a small rounded (i.e. skull-shaped)
hill 'nigh to the city,' at present unidentified. Our word
'Calvary' comes from the Vulgate translation of the explanatory
phrase (*calvariae locus*).

23. mingled with myrrh. A draught to deaden pain, given
to condemned criminals, and prepared by the women of Jerusalem
(cf. Luke xxiii. 27). Matt. (xxvii. 34) says that He refused it
after tasting the draught. He would not forego any part of the
suffering, that His submission might be complete. The draught
of sour wine (36) would not have any such deadening effect.

24. crucify. This form of execution was too familiar to

casting lots upon them, what each should take. And it 25
was the third hour, and they crucified him. And the 26
superscription of his accusation was written over, THE
KING OF THE JEWS. And with him they crucify two 27
robbers; one on his right hand, and one on his left. And 29
they that passed by railed on him, wagging their heads,
and saying, Ha! thou that destroyest the temple, and
buildest it in three days, save thyself, and come down 30
from the cross. In like manner also the chief priests 31
mocking *him* among themselves with the scribes said,

---

need description. The shape of the cross is uncertain, but since
there was an inscription (which would be attached to an upright),
it was probably a 'Latin' cross. John tells us that there
were four men charged with the execution, and he gives further
details of their actions, pointing out the fulfilment of Ps. xxii. 18.
The dice had been brought to while away the hours of waiting
for the death.

25. third hour. Reckoning from the average time of 'dawn.'
John puts the end of the Roman Trial at 'about the sixth
hour': at present his statements as to the day and hour of
the Crucifixion have not been satisfactorily reconciled with those
in the synoptic Gospels.

26. superscription. It was usual to write the name and
crime of a condemned man on a board, carried with him to the
place of execution. In Latin the inscription here given probably
ran thus: IESUS · NAZARENUS · REX · IUDAEORUM
(whence the initials INRI often seen in pictures), the first two
words giving the name, the last two the 'crime' (see John xix.
21, 22). It was also given in Aramaic and Greek, for the
benefit of Jews from all parts.

27. two robbers. See Luke xxii. 32, 39-43; Matt. xxvii.
38, 44; John xix. 18. Possibly these were followers of Barabbas.
(Cf. here the A.V. (28) which gives a quotation from Is. liii.
12.)

29. passed by, i.e. going to or returning from the town,
along the road. These mockers had heard of the evidence at
the Jewish Trial (n. on xiv. 58).

30. They had also heard of His answer to Caiaphas (xiv. 61,
62) as Matt.'s account shows (xxvii. 40). He adds the words
"If Thou be the Son of God."

31. among themselves, i.e. not joining in the vulgar loud
mockery.

32 He saved others; himself he cannot save. Let the Christ, the King of Israel, now come down from the cross, that we may see and believe. And they that were crucified with him reproached him.

33 And when the sixth hour was come, there was darkness
34 over the whole land until the ninth hour. And at the ninth hour Jesus cried with a loud voice, Eloi, Eloi, lama sabachthani? which is, being interpreted, My God, my
35 God, why hast thou forsaken me? And some of them that stood by, when they heard it, said, Behold, he calleth
36 Elijah. And one ran, and filling a sponge full of vinegar, put it on a reed, and gave him to drink, saying, Let be;
37 let us see whether Elijah cometh to take him down. And

---

he saved others. They admit His works of mercy. Perhaps also there is a mocking allusion to His name, Jesus (Saviour).

32. The priests, having tried in vain to induce Pilate to alter the inscription (John xix. 21, 22), now quote it in mockery, altering the wording to make it fit in with their own ideas of the Messiah.

reproached him. Luke adds that one of the two rebuked the other for doing this, and received comfort from Jesus.

33. the sixth hour, i.e. mid-day.

darkness. Its nature and extent are not explained.

the whole land, i.e. Judaea.

34. The only one of the 'seven last words' recorded by Mark or Matt.: the other six are given by Luke and John. The original Aramaic is given: the words are quoted from Ps. xxii. 1, and mark the final stage in the sufferings endured. The sayings recorded Luke xxiii. 46, John xix. 30, mark the final victory.

35. Either these were Greek-speaking Jews who did not know Aramaic, or else they wilfully played on the word, an improbable piece of irreverence. The Jews expected the return of Elijah (vi. 15), and he was also regarded as a great deliverer.

36. vinegar. The sour wine drunk by the common folk, and brought apparently by the soldiers for their own use (see John xix. 29). John also tells us that Jesus said "I thirst." This drink would not deaden His consciousness or sense of pain (see 23); it would rather give Him the fuller use of His faculties, and His words testified to the *reality* of His humanity.

to drink. Apparently an allusion to Ps. lxix. 21.

saying. Matt. gives the words to the bystanders.

Jesus uttered a loud voice, and gave up the ghost. And 38 the veil of the temple was rent in twain from the top to the bottom. And when the centurion, which stood by 39 over against him, saw that he so gave up the ghost, he said, Truly this man was the Son of God. And there 40 were also women beholding from afar: among whom *were* both Mary Magdalene, and Mary the mother of James the less and of Joses, and Salome; who, when he 41

---

37. a loud voice. Probably the cry "Father, into thy hands I commend my spirit" (Luke xxiii. 46): John's "It is finished" (xix. 30) must have been uttered just before this, and was perhaps heard only by those (like John) who stood close to the Cross. The Sufferer by a strong effort of will maintained His full consciousness to the last. The death occurred unexpectedly soon, (see 44, and cf. John xix. 31–34), probably hastened by the intense mental anguish.

38. the veil…was rent, thus symbolizing the passing away of the Old Covenant. The 'veil' covered the entrance to the Holy of Holies.

39. the centurion. Tradition names him Longinus: he was in command of the Roman soldiers, and therefore on duty in front of the crosses.

40. Cf. this verse with A.V. The impression was made by Jesus' whole bearing on the Cross, and by the signs which attended His death.

the Son of God. The centurion meant probably 'more than an ordinary man': Luke says 'a righteous man.'

40. women. The first two named here are mentioned again in 47, and all three in xvi. 1.

from afar, i.e. at a safe distance from the scoffing soldiers.

Magdalene, i.e. 'of Magdala,' a town on the Sea of Galilee: she had been freed by Jesus from seven devils (Luke viii. 2) and had given Him of her substance. There is no ground for identifying her with the "woman which was a sinner" (Luke vii. 37).

the mother of James. She is generally identified with the "Mary the *wife* (?) of Clopas" mentioned by John (xix. 25), and it is supposed that Clopas and Alphaeus are different forms of the same name. If so, 'James the Little' was the same as James 'son of Alphaeus' who was one of the Twelve (n. on iii. 18).

Joses, not of course the same as he who was 'brother' of the Lord (vi. 3).

Salome, wife of Zebedee, and mother of James and John:

was in Galilee, followed him, and ministered, unto him;
and many other women which came up with him unto
Jerusalem.

42   And when even was now come, because it was the
43 Preparation, that is, the day before the sabbath, there
came Joseph of Arimathæa, a councillor of honourable
estate, who also himself was looking for the kingdom of
God ; and he boldly went in unto Pilate, and asked for
44 the body of Jesus. And Pilate marvelled if he were
already dead : and calling unto him the centurion, he
45 asked him whether he had been any while dead. And
46 when he learned it of the centurion, he granted the corpse

---

probably she was the Virgin Mary's sister (see John xix. 25).
This would explain Jesus' charge to John from the Cross (John
xix. 26, 27).   See also Matt. xx. 20.

41.   many other women. See the list given by Luke (viii. 2).

42.   even = ' late afternoon ' as in iv. 35.

the Preparation, i.e. the eve of the Passover : the word
(explained here for Gentile readers) had become a regular word
for our 'Friday.'

43.   Arimathæa, generally identified with Ramathaim, Sa-
muel's birthplace (1 Sam. i. 1).

a councillor, i.e. a member of the Sanhedrin.   Luke tells us
(xxiii. 50, 51) that he had not voted for Jesus' condemnation.
Cf. the description of his attitude with that of Simeon (Luke ii.
25).   They were both amongst those who expected the immediate coming of the Messiah's kingdom.   Joseph had become
a secret disciple of Jesus (John xix. 38).

boldly. This touch is peculiar to Mark, and may be due to
Peter, who thus emphasized a contrast with his own cowardice. It
was a contrast too with Nicodemus' own visit to the Lord by night
(John iii.).   The bodies of crucified criminals were cast into a
common grave, often after an interval of some days, but the
Romans allowed the Jews to claim their own because their law
forbade a man to hang all night upon a tree.   On this occasion
there was the extra reason that the next day was the Sabbath.

44.   marvelled, nn. on 15, 37.   Crucifixion would not
ordinarily cause death in a few hours ; a lingering death from
starvation would be more usual.

45.   he learned it, i.e. when the death was officially con-
firmed.

the corpse, a word used specially of the 'carcases' of animals:

to Joseph. And he bought a linen cloth, and taking him 46
down, wound him in the linen cloth, and laid him in a
tomb which had been hewn out of a rock; and he rolled
a stone against the door of the tomb. And Mary Mag- 47
dalene and Mary the *mother* of Joses beheld where he
was laid

XVI. 1–8.

CONCLUSION : THE RESURRECTION.

1–8. *The women's visit to the tomb.*

And when the sabbath was past, Mary Magdalene, and **16**
Mary the *mother* of James, and Salome, bought spices,
that they might come and anoint him. And very early **2**
on the first day of the week, they come to the tomb when

---

probably the contemptuous phrase of Pilate for the Body. It is
however used in vi. 29 for a 'corpse.'
46. wound him, helped by Nicodemus, who brought materials
for embalming (John xix. 39).
a tomb. Rock-hewn for Joseph himself in his own garden.
Two Jewish kings (Manasseh and Amon) are said to have been
buried in the garden of the palace (2 Kings xxi. 18, 26).
47. This sentence explains the next incident.

1–8. *The women's visit to the tomb.*
[*Matt. xxviii.* 1–8. *Luke xxiv.* 1–11. *John xx.* 1–11.]

XVI. 1. was past, i.e. after sunset on the Sabbath. The
same women who were mentioned in xv. 40, come now to the
tomb. John records Mary of Magdala's visit *alone* to the tomb
as the first visit. Possibly she went on ahead, and left the tomb
before the other women reached it. But, as John relates incidents not recorded by the Synoptists, while they do not aim at
a complete account, it is impossible to construct a continuous
narrative of the Resurrection, harmonising all the incidents[1].
anoint him, remembering probably His words at Bethany
(xiv. 8).
2. very early, i.e. starting at early dawn, and arriving after
sunrise.

[1] For a suggested harmony see Westcott's *S. John*, p. 288.

CH.   8

3 the sun was risen. And they were saying among themselves, Who shall roll us away the stone from the door
4 of the tomb? and looking up, they see that the stone is
5 rolled back: for it was exceeding great. And entering
into the tomb, they saw a young man sitting on the right
side, arrayed in a white robe; and they were amazed.
6 And he saith unto them, Be not amazed: ye seek Jesus,
the Nazarene, which hath been crucified: he is risen; he
7 is not here: behold, the place where they laid him! But
go, tell his disciples and Peter, He goeth before you into
8 Galilee: there shall ye see him, as he said unto you. And
they went out, and fled from the tomb; for trembling and
astonishment had come upon them: and they said nothing
to any one; for they were afraid.

3, 4. were saying, i.e. as they went along: then 'looking
up' to the hillside out of which the tomb was cut they saw that
the stone had been moved. (Cf. this graphic rendering of the
R.V. with the past tenses of the A.V.)

rolled back (cf. A.V.). The stone was not gone, only moved
aside so as to clear the entrance[1]. It could be seen *from afar*,
"for it was exceeding great."

5. Matt.'s account differs in the details, but all the evangelists
agree in these main outlines :—That the first visit to the tomb was
made by the *women*, That the first sign of the Resurrection
was the removal of the *stone*, That a vision of *angels* appeared to
the women before anyone had seen Jesus Himself, That He was
first seen by Mary of Magdala. The independence of the Gospels is thus well illustrated by the story of the Resurrection. See
Introd. p. ix.

7. and Peter, both as the chief of the Apostles and because
of his recent fall. His forgiveness is implied, and full àssurance
of this is recorded by John.

into Galilee. As He had told them after the Supper (xiv. 28).
The message would dispel any false ideas of a great manifestation
in Jerusalem.

8. they were afraid. Here the Gospel in its earliest form
ends with singular abruptness, and with an incomplete sentence
(in the Greek). Either some accident prevented its conclusion,
or a leaf of the original copy may have been lost[2].

---

[1] Latham, *The Risen Master*, chap. i. and illustration.
[2] W. H., II. notes, p. 47.

XVI. 9–20.

[APPENDED SUMMARY ON THE RESURRECTION.]

Appearances to Mary Magdalene; to the Disciples; to the Eleven.

Now when he was risen early on the first day of the 9
week, he appeared first to Mary Magdalene, from whom
he had cast out seven devils. She went and told them 10
that had been with him, as they mourned and wept. And 11
they, when they heard that he was alive, and had been
seen of her, disbelieved.

And after these things he was manifested in another 12

Appearances to Mary Magdalene; to the Disciples; to the Eleven.

[*Matt. xxviii.* 9–20. *Luke xxiv.* 12–52. *John xx.* 12–29.]

9–20. This passage is probably a very early addition to the
Gospel. The change of subject (between 8 and 9) is extremely
abrupt, and the style is quite unlike that of Mark. Instead of a
narrative we have here a brief summary of events covering a
considerable period, and the writer shows a strong desire to
'point a moral,' insisting frequently on the unbelief of the
disciples. This trait is not in the least characteristic of Mark.

In 1891 was discovered an Armenian MS. of the Gospels,
which states that this passage was written by 'the presbyter
Ariston': an early authority tells us that one Aristion was a
disciple of the Lord, but this is all we know of such a person.

9–11. This first appearance is recorded by John (xx. 11–18).

9. The construction of this verse (in the Greek) shows that
the passage has been transferred from some other context. The
note of time given is unnecessary in *this* context, after *v.* 2.

Mary Magdalene. Mentioned as if for the first time (see 1–8).
The statement here made agrees with that in John xx. 11, but
hardly with that in 1–8 of this chapter. The cure referred to
here is mentioned also by Luke (viii. 2) but is not related at
length anywhere. St Paul's list of the witnesses of the Resurrection does not include Mary of Magdala (1 Cor. xv. 5–8).

10. them that had been with him, i.e. strictly the Eleven;
but others were also present (Acts i. 13, 14).

11. seen. The verb implies more than mere seeing, it means
to 'gaze,' as on some great sight. John (xx. 18) omits mention
of the disciples' unbelief.

12, 13. This is the appearance to two disciples walking to
Emmaus, a village about 7 m. from Jerusalem, later in the day
of the Resurrection (see Luke xxiv. 13–32).

form unto two of them, as they walked, on their way into
13 the country. And they went away and told it unto the
rest: neither believed they them.

14 And afterward he was manifested unto the eleven themselves as they sat at meat; and he upbraided them with
their unbelief and hardness of heart, because they believed
15 not them which had seen him after he was risen. And he
said unto them, Go ye into all the world, and preach the
16 gospel to the whole creation. He that believeth and is
baptized shall be saved; but he that disbelieveth shall
17 be condemned. And these signs shall follow them that
believe: in my name shall they cast out devils; they shall

---

12. in another form, i.e. not as He had appeared to Mary of
Magdala, who thought He was a gardener (John xx. 15): these
took Him for an ordinary traveller. In some way His form was
unfamiliar.

two of them, i.e. two of the company 'that had been with him.'
Luke gives the name of one of them as Cleopas.

13. neither believed they. Cf. Luke's conflicting account
(xxiv. 34). Probably not all had believed Peter's report, and
these would refuse also the testimony of the Two.

14-18. A brief summary of the various appearances to the
whole body of the disciples. Luke gives one such appearance
at Jerusalem, John two, at an interval of a week: others (which
may or may not have been in Jerusalem) are recorded by Matt.,
John, and St Paul (1 Cor. xv. 5). The vague word **afterward**
is used to group various appearances together. Throughout this
summary the writer insists on the unbelief of the disciples: this
does not seem to agree with Luke or John, but the writer dates
the occasion too vaguely for exact comparison.

upbraided. An unusually strong term of rebuke.

15. A very sudden change from severe rebuke to this solemn
charge to preach the Gospel everywhere. Possibly these words
belong to a later occasion, such as the appearance in Galilee
recorded by Matt. (xxviii. 16-20).

the whole creation, i.e. 'all the nations' (Matt. xxviii. 19).
The phrase suggests St Paul's teaching of the redemption of *all
nature*, cf. Col. i. 23; Rom. viii. 22

16. disbelieveth. Note the prominence given to 'unbelief'
in this whole passage (8-20), cf. 11, 13, 14. This may explain
why the writer inserts here this charge with its warnings 15-18.

condemned. What his 'condemnation' will be is not stated.

speak with new tongues; they shall take up serpents, and 18
if they drink any deadly thing, it shall in no wise hurt
them; they shall lay hands on the sick, and they shall
recover.

So then the Lord Jesus, after he had spoken unto them, 19
was received up into heaven, and sat down at the right
hand of God. And they went forth, and preached every- 20
where, the Lord working with them, and confirming the
word by the signs that followed. Amen.

---

17. with new tongues. The first instance of this 'sign' is the
Day of Pentecost (Acts ii.). It often occurs later in the N.T.:
see St Paul's discussion in 1 Cor. xiv. The exact nature of the
gift is uncertain. See Art. 'Gift of Tongues' in Smith's *Bible
Dict.*

18. take up serpents. Cf. Ps. xci. 13. A 'sign' foretold to
the Seventy (Luke x. 19). Cf. Acts xxviii. 3–5.

lay hands on the sick. A symbolical act used by Jesus Himself in healing, but not by His disciples till after the Ascension.
See Acts ix. 12, xxviii. 8.

19. after he had spoken. A vague note of time. The
statement which follows is quite unlike the style of the evangelists,
who record what the disciples *saw*. Here (in the last clause) the
writer gives his *belief*, and the phrase sounds like the fragment
of an early creed. Note also the unusual phrase 'the Lord Jesus.'

at the right hand, n. on xii. 36.

20. A summary of the missionary labours of the disciples: cf.
Heb. ii. 4.

went forth, from Jerusalem, their original centre.

Some ancient texts give (instead of 9–20) a different ending to the
Gospel. "And they briefly reported to Peter and those with him
all that had been told them. And after these things even Jesus
Himself sent out by means of them from the east even to the west
the sacred and incorruptible proclamation of eternal salvation."

Westcott and Hort include this 'alternative ending' in their
text, while placing it in double brackets to mark it as a later
addition. They explain it thus: "It was [probably] appended
by a scribe or editor who knew no other ending to the Gospel
than *v.* 8, was offended with its abruptness, and completed the
broken sentence by a summary of the contents of St Luke xxiv.
9–12, and the Gospel by a comprehensive sentence suggested
probably by Matt. xxviii. 19; Luke xxiv. 47; John xx. 21."[1]

[1] W. H. II. *notes,* p. 44.

INDEX

Abba, 98
Abiathar, 15
'Abomination of desolation,' 88
Agony in the garden, 98
Alabaster cruse, 92
Alexander, 108
Alphaeus, 12, 19, 111
Analysis of Gospel, xxviii
Angels, 4
Annas, 101
Apostles, meaning of word, 17; mission of, 33
Appearances of Jesus, 114, 115, 116
Aramaic, 31, 43, 46, 98, 110
Arrest of Jesus, 100
Ascension, 117
Ass, 72

Baptism, of John, 2; of Our Lord, 3; referred to, 68, 116
Barabbas, 106
Barnabas, xii
Bartholomew, 18
Bartimaeus, 70
Baskets, words used for, 39, 48
Beelzebub, 19
Bethany, 71, 92
Bethphage, 71
Bethsaida, 39, 50
Betrayal of Jesus, 100
Blasphemy against the Holy Ghost, 20; charge of, 103
Blindness cured, 50, 70
'Brethren of the Lord,' 20, 32
'Bride-chamber, children of the,' 13

Caesar, 80
Caesarea Philippi, 51
Caiaphas, 101

Calvary, 108
Camel's hair, 2
Cananaean, Simon the, 19
Capernaum, 6
Centurion, 111
'Chief priests,' explanation of, 51
'Chief seats,' 84
Christ, meaning of name, 1
Cleansing of the Temple, 74
Cleopas, 116
Commandments, the, 64, 82
Corn, plucking ears of, 14
Corban, 43
'Corner, head of the,' 79
Covenant, blood of the, 96
Covetousness, 44
Crown of thorns, 107
Crucifixion, the, 108
'Cup,' meaning of, 68; Cup of Blessing, 96

Dalmanutha, 48
David, 15; son of, 83
Decapolis, 29
Demoniacs, explanation, 6; healing of, 7, 27, 57
Denarius, 38, 80
Disciples, meaning of word, 17; call of, 12, 16, 17
Divorce, question concerning, 62

Emmaus, appearance on way to, 116
Ephphatha, 46

Fasting, Jewish rules of, 13
Faith, lesson on, 75
Fig tree, withering of, 74; parable of, 90

Fire, purification by, 61
Five thousand, feeding of, 37
Four thousand, feeding of, 47

Galilee, tour in, 4; dialect of, 104; apostles sent there, 114
Gehenna, 60
Gennesaret, plain of, 41
Gerasenes, Gergesa, 27
Gethsemane, 97
Ghost, the Holy, blasphemy against, 20; descent of, 3; promise of, 87
Golgotha, 108
Gospel, meaning of, 1
Greek, a, 45
Guard, soldier of the, 36

'Head of the corner, the,' 79
Hell, 60
Herod Antipas, xxiii, 35, 107
Herodians, the, 16, 79
Herodias, 35
High priest, 51
Holy Ghost, descent of, 3; blasphemy against, 20; promise of, 87

Idumaea, 16
Inscription on the Cross, 109

Jairus, daughter of, restored to life, 29
James, surnamed with John Boanerges, 6, 18, 31, 54, 68, 98
James the son of Alphaeus, 18, 111
Jericho, history of, 70; blind man healed at, 71
Jerusalem, triumphal entry into, 72; prophecies concerning, 85, 89
JESUS:
    Name, 1; Baptism, 3; Temptation, 4; Ministry in Eastern Galilee begins, 4; in Northern Galilee,

45; in Peraea and Judaea, 62; the Last Week, 71; the Crucifixion, 109; Burial, 113; Resurrection, 114; Appearances, 115, 116; Ascension, 117
John, brother of James, call of, 6, 18, 31, 54, 68, 98
John the Baptist, 2, 3, 35, 51
Joseph of Arimathaea, 112
Joseph, the husband of Mary, 32
Judas Iscariot, his call, 19; his avarice, 92, 93; his treachery, 99
Judas, surnamed Thaddaeus, 18

'Kingdom of God,' meaning of phrase, 5; parables concerning, 21–25; misconception of, 65

Latchet, 2
Leaven, of the Pharisees and of Herod, 49
Leper, cleansing of, 8
Levi, call of, 12
Locusts, 2

Magdalene, *see* Mary
Malchus, 100
'Man, Son of,' 11
Mark, his life, xi–xiv; his Gospel, xiv–xvi
Marriage, questions concerning, 62, 81
Mary Magdalene, 111, 113, 115
Mary, the Virgin, 21
Mary of Bethany, 92
Mary the mother of James, 111, 113
Matthew, call of, 12
Messiah, popular expectation of, 51, 53, 65, 68
Mite, the widow's, 85
Mustard Seed, parable of, 25
'Mystery, the,' 22

Nathanael, call of, 18
Nazareth, 3; rejection at, 32
New Cloth and New Wine, parables of, 14
Nicodemus, 113

Parable, meaning of word, 19
Paralytic, healing of, 10
Passover, the, 93
Penny, value of, 38, 92
Peter, call of, 5; his mother-in-law healed, 7; present on three great occasions, 31, 54, 98; his confession and presumption, 51, 52; his denial, 97, 104; message to, 114; relations to Mark, xvi
Pharisees, sect of, 12; hostility of, 14, 16, 79; denunciation of, 49, 84
Philip, call of, 18
Pilate, trial before, 105; consents to Joseph's request, 112
Praetorium, 105, 107
Prayer, teaching on, 76
Publicans, explanation of, 12
Purple, the royal mantle, 107

Rabboni, 70
Resurrection, the, 114
Roofs, how constructed in Palestine, 10
Ruler of Synagogue, 29

Sabbath, teaching concerning, 15, 16; miracles wrought on, 7, 8, 16
Sadducees, 49, 81
Salome, mother of James and John, 68, 111
Salome, daughter of Herodias, 36
Sanhedrin, the, 101, 105

Satan, temptation by, 4
Scourging, Roman torture of, 107
Scribes, see Pharisees; their teaching, 6
Simon of Cyrene, 108
Simon Peter, see Peter
Simon the Zealot, call of, 5; name explained, 18
Simon the leper, 92
Son of man, meaning of phrase, 11
Sower, the parable of, 24
Supper, the Last, 94
Swine, destruction of, 28
Synagogue, how used, 6; Jesus teaches in, 6; rulers of, 29
Syrophoenician woman, the, 45

Talitha Cumi, 31
Temple, the, cleansing of, 74; prophecies concerning, 85; veil rent, 111
Temptation, the, 4
Thaddaeus, call of, 19
Thomas, call of, 19
Thorns, crown of, 107
Title on the Cross, 109
Tombs cut in the rock, 27, 113
Transfiguration, the, 54
Treasure-chests in the Temple, 84
Tribute to Caesar, 80
Triumphal entry, 72
Tyre, borders of, 45

Voice heard from heaven, 3, 55

Watches of the night, 40
Widow's offering, 85

Zealot, Simon the, 5, 18
Zebedee, 6